Praise

Every leader could benefit from the practical approach to decision making set out in this book. Too often, important decisions in business get settled by who yells the loudest. Paul's very practical book shows you how to manage decision processes in a better way that will generate the best outcomes for your organisation and get the buy in from the team so that things actually get implemented.

— **Patrick Sharry**, AGSM Fellow, University of New South Wales

A superbly crafted book that is intensely practical and theoretically sound, with many real case studies!

— **Lawrence D Phillips**, Emeritus Professor of Decision Sciences, London School of Economics & Political Science

His findings and approach are common sense. They are practical and applicable. I recommend them.

— **Rhys Jones**, Lieutenant General (Retired), Former Chief of Defence, New Zealand Defence Force

Hard decisions made easy

How leaders in large
organisations make complex
decisions that stick

PAUL GORDON

Re think

First published in Great Britain in 2021
by Rethink Press (www.rethinkpress.com)

© Copyright Paul Gordon

*For Dad; one of the greatest decision-makers
I've ever known.*

I miss you.

Contents

Foreword   1

Introduction   5

1 **The Case For Better Decision Making**   9

   Typical decision making   9

   What is better decision making?   13

   Why 'better' decision making?   14

   Why do people think that better decision making is hard?   16

   Gut feeling is no longer enough   19

   Bridging the strategy-execution gap   21

   Governance is not decision making   22

   Avoiding pitfalls   24

   Reflection   25

   Summary   26

2 The P⁵ Decision Framework   **29**

Underlying principles   29

Core components of the P⁵ Decision
Framework   38

Avoiding pitfalls   43

Reflection   44

Summary   45

3 Plan   **47**

Setting up for success   47

Questions to ask in the Plan phase   50

Foundations of the Plan phase   54

Planning in practice   56

Avoiding pitfalls   60

Reflection   62

Summary   63

4 Prepare Value   **65**

What is value?   65

Value is more than just money   67

Questions to ask in the Prepare Value phase   69

Foundations of the Prepare Value phase   71

Prepare Value in practice   73

Attributes of good criteria   75

Avoiding pitfalls   80

Reflection   82

Summary   82

5 **Prepare Alternatives**   **85**

What does a good alternative look like?   85

Types of alternatives   87

Questions to ask in the Prepare
Alternatives phase   91

Foundations of the Prepare
Alternatives phase   91

How to develop alternatives   94

What data do we need?   96

Avoiding pitfalls   100

Reflection   101

Summary   102

6 **Prioritise**   **103**

Why prioritise?   103

Questions to ask in the Prioritise phase   104

Foundations of the Prioritise phase   105

Prioritisation in practice   106

Evaluating alternatives –
the technical process   107

Order of priority and sensitivity analysis   113

Decision Conferencing – the social process   116

Decision Conferencing in practice   117

Avoiding pitfalls 124

Reflection 125

Summary 126

7 Package **129**

Why package? 129

The core inputs to the Package phase 131

Constraints versus criteria in
decision making 132

Understanding value for money 134

Questions to ask during the Package phase 135

Foundations of the Package phase 136

Making trade-offs 137

Packaging in summary 138

Packaging in practice 140

Avoiding pitfalls 149

Reflection 150

Summary 150

8 Present **153**

Why present? 153

Questions to ask in the Present phase 155

Foundations of the Present phase 156

Present in practice 157

Avoiding pitfalls 165

Reflection 166

Summary 167

Conclusion 169

What action can you take right now? 172

References 175

Acknowledgements 179

The Author 183

Foreword

The ability for organisations to make good decisions on investment or other matters revolves around their capacity to identify and compare not only cost but also value and, ultimately, benefits. Value is more important than simply cost in most decisions but is the harder of the two to define and compare. The value might fall on different parts of the organisation or not be quantifiable in financial terms, whereas cost is more easily defined in the short and long terms. Critically, greater cost does not equal greater value, and there is the truism that squeezing out the last 5% of value will cost far more than 5% of the total cost.

Usually, as organisations and businesses grow and mature, the decision-making requirements become more complex. Early in the life of an organisation decisions are primarily based around establishing the core business – the production process or the service provided. These decisions are reasonably simple – will this investment increase capacity, widen capability and increase profit? How will investment option A compare in these matters to investment options B, C and D?

However, sooner or later organisations will face less easily comparable options. Should we continue to invest in growing our current capability or should we invest in research and development to seek an innovative improvement? Should we invest in upgrading equipment that will improve output or should we invest in staff development to have lower staff turnover and therefore build a more experienced and productive workforce? If we invest in one thing, what are the opportunity costs of not investing in something else? Where will the main benefits fall?

The need for managers and leaders to be able to handle such complexity is not new but it can be the difference between an organisation sinking, floating or moving ahead. Experience alone will not guarantee success, so the ability to generate good decision-making processes and practices and to engage the right people in the consideration is a huge advantage to any organisation.

I first encountered Paul Gordon and his decision framework, including multi-criteria decision analysis, when I worked as the head of the Defence Force Development Branch. That branch was responsible for working alongside the New Zealand Ministry of Defence for capital investment programmes over $10 million and was totally responsible for the portfolio and programme management of the Defence Force's capital investments of under $10 million. There were, of course, more projects being proposed than there was money to spend so there was a need to have an effective process to compare the choices, when the focus of each one was so different.

Building on the experience that was gained through this process, the Defence Force engaged with Paul on ever more complex issues and with much wider interest groups involved, culminating in the midpoint rebalancing review, mentioned in this book. Having a credible and trusted process as the guide through these considerations not only gave the Defence Force an agreed process to balance the competing priorities of the Navy, Army and Air Force, but most importantly it reassured the Treasury and political stakeholders that there was a transparent and robust process being used. The confidence that such a process provided to the ultimate decision-makers was the key to the success of the review.

No 'robust' process is fast and easy and continual short-cutting of the system will eventually undermine internal and external confidence in the process. Familiarity through constant use for small and large decision processes is recommended. Confidence and proficiency will flow, delivering sound decisions and a more coherent organisation, rather than one divided by competing priorities and perspectives. There will still be tough decisions to make amid changing priorities and external pressures. However, the organisation having trust in its decision-making tools is an essential element in internal and external confidence.

This book is here to help organisations and leaders make the right decisions. Paul Gordon gives you the benefit of his experience of working with organisations to establish, run and be proficient in the processes of correctly identifying the right factors to consider and who to involve. His findings and approach are common sense. They are practical and applicable. I recommend them.

Rhys Jones, Lieutenant General (Retired), Former Chief of Defence, New Zealand Defence Force

Introduction

I started life as a software engineer and became fascinated with the way people in large organisations made decisions. I realised that decision making makes the world go round and I took up the challenge to transform the way the world makes decisions that matter. I wrote this book because I was frustrated at organisations who made decisions badly that then led to poor outcomes with disengaged stakeholders. They had no idea that there was a structured, rigorous way of making decisions that stick. In my work at Catalyze, I've been helping organisations like 3M, Woodside, the New Zealand Defence Force, the New Zealand Police, the Australian Federal Department of Finance and the Australian Department of Defence to do so for more than fifteen years and, in my mind, I've been researching this book all that time. I bring together mine and my colleagues' decades of experience from the UK, New Zealand and Australia, where we have worked with hundreds of large organisations across the public and private sectors, helping them make hard decisions in complex environments with many stakeholders, with strong commitment to the outcome – to make decisions that stick.

Even after all these years, it surprises me that people and organisations are still making decisions poorly, and I'm committed to addressing this. This book articulates the work my colleagues and I have been doing so that, wherever you are, you can gain from our experience, and not make the myriad mistakes I've seen being made elsewhere in the world.

If you're someone who is making decisions worth millions or even billions of dollars, or you have been delegated to make decisions of this kind, you are likely to be a senior leader or a general manager in a large organisation such as a government department or a global multi-national corporation. If you identify with either scenario, this book is for you.

We will explore a set of core principles that will improve the quality of your and your organisation's decision making, whether that is a decision on where to set up your next office or on which warship to buy.

If you read this book fully, you will find a clear way through making complex decisions and having them endure. You will learn about a robust framework for decision making, underpinned by a set of core principles – the P^5 Decision Framework. This is a practical and pragmatic framework that has been distilled from mine and my colleagues' years of practical experience and has been tried and tested. You will read real-life examples in each chapter that bring the framework alive and relate it to the world you're coming from. I'll highlight key pitfalls so that you can avoid what doesn't work.

The great news is that decision making is, itself, a discipline and all problems can be solved with a structured decision-making approach – the emerging discipline of Decision Thinking. Therefore, this book is the answer to that age-old question: 'How do I make that decision?' More importantly, it also answers the question: 'How do I make that decision stick?' It brings together my experience and thinking into a five-phase rigorous framework:

1. **Plan:** getting your act together.

2. **Prepare:** bringing together the key inputs to your decision.

3. **Prioritise:** prioritising your alternatives.

4. **Package:** turning your alternatives into reality.

5. **Present:** taking your decision to the ultimate authority for commitment.

By reading the book you will get the full picture of the P^5 Framework, see how the principles and the framework fit together and gain insight into every aspect of decision making. A Reflection section is added at the end of each chapter so that you can apply the content to whatever decision you are making. Worksheets and an online diagnostic tool have also been provided at the end of the book, which will help in quality-checking the decisions you are making. Throughout the book I will provide real-world case studies to illustrate different aspects of better decision making. In addition, to help you navigate through the book, I will refer to a single, common, real-world case study – the story of a client, 'Jane', the chief information officer (CIO) of a large district health board.

Keep the book to hand; if you find you are challenged by a complex decision with multiple stakeholders, you may find the answers that will help you move forward by reading the relevant chapter.

1
The Case For Better Decision Making

Typical decision making

Let's start by looking at complex or big decisions. These are decisions that affect many people and involve millions of dollars. They are large financial investments and have multiple consequences with different objectives that need to be considered. An example could be: where is the best place to store nuclear waste? What is the right balance of capital investments to make and which investments should not be made? What configuration of warship should be bought? You might want to decide the right location for your company headquarters or be considering how you will deliver your five-year company vision. This book is concerned with this scale of decision making. It's not about deciding whether to wear a red or blue shirt today, nor is it about whether a decision is a good or bad one. Our focus will be on the difference between effective and ineffective decision making. We're here to look at what works and what doesn't work, why it works and why it doesn't work. Let's start by considering how decisions are typically made.

Usually, in large organisations, a senior leader or 'sponsor' makes the important decisions. There might be a defined process to get something signed off but it typically starts with a group of people posturing around the water cooler or with the chosen few having a conversation over a barbecue. Maybe other people hear about it and stick their oar in, saying, 'You really need to go this way.' Then there are those who want it to go a different way and shout the loudest or thump the table. If you're lucky, there will be consultation with stakeholders such as customers or shareholders in the form of a focus group or a stakeholder survey. There is rarely proper consideration of the stakeholders' perspective. Most commonly the discussion is about the wrong things with the wrong people and with no deliberate process.

All of this gives an unstructured randomness to decision making, with the emphasis on the accountable decision-maker trying to get their way using the nicest and quickest means possible. This book is not intended to be controversial or provocative. It's here to shine a light on some of the things that can go on. An organisation I know said their process was DAD (decide, announce, defend) and this is common. Someone makes a decision and then stands their ground in the face of challenges.

What's wrong with decision making like this?

- Decisions don't stick. They either don't get executed or they get turned over down the track. If your decision isn't going to get executed or endure, there is no point making it – hence the subtitle of this book.

- Decisions take a lot longer than people think. They might say that they will have a chat with a few people and then come to a decision, but this takes time.

- Decisions don't stand up to scrutiny from shareholders in the private sector or from the public purse in the public sector, and organisations lose the trust of their stakeholders, especially where high-impact decisions are concerned. This leads to re-contesting and a re-examination of why the decision was made and whether it was the right decision. This all takes time and money and frequently doesn't deliver the outcome intended.

- Often organisations don't distinguish between the decision and its outcome. As busy leaders and executives, our KPIs (key performance indicators) relate to how we spent our budget or whether decisions were made on time. They are not about what the decision leads to. Emphasis is placed on getting to a decision but, frankly, you could toss a coin and that will give you a decision. The challenge is getting it executed.

- Poor decision making doesn't drive what matters in terms of company performance. Company performance may well look like greater customer satisfaction, better competitiveness or improved environmental sustainability, but the typical way decisions are made doesn't result in this. It might turn out some good dollar numbers, but all other things get left behind.

CASE STUDY – HOW TO TURN A BUSINESS AROUND

A UK subsidiary of a global corporation faced diminishing profit and experienced what they called 'negative growth'. They realised that their different business units were doing what they'd always done and were chasing their tail to stay alive. Each business unit was operating in isolation of the others – as true 'silos'.

They put in place a structured decision-making process, using the five phases of the P^5 Framework. This caused them to look across the business and consider every single product line. By understanding how each product line delivered on what was important for the business – revenue, profit, innovation, customer satisfaction, etc – they were able to discontinue some product lines, scale down other activities and, crucially, scale up activities that were going to help them win. With this greater transparency and visibility, and with engagement of the entire organisation, they agreed a way forward and executed on it.

Within two years they went from negative growth to an additional £300 million on their bottom line. The keys to this success were engagement across the organisation, rigorous and structured consideration of all possible activities (both divestments and investments) and a clear focus on what was important for the business – in this case, much more than just profit.

What is better decision making?

Better decision making includes:

- Increased transparency – a greater visibility of what's going on for all the people concerned. This will give consistency in how decisions are made.

- A scientifically grounded process that underpins the decision.

- A structure that makes it clear how the decision progresses.

- Active stakeholder engagement, which enables them to participate in the decision.

- Delivering all the outcomes required, not just the financial ones.

- Decisions that are executed and that endure.

This is what better decision making can look like at the highest level. This is Decision Thinking: conscious, structured, transparent, collaborative decision making. This book will explore how this can work in practice.

Why 'better' decision making?

Let's consider what better decision making can deliver, once these decisions stick.

Firstly, it drives greater organisational performance and results. One of the typical failures of decision-making processes is that they don't deliver the outcome. In this world of increased visibility, CEOs are scared about their reputation and are highly focused on driving share prices up. There's nothing worse for reputation than a big decision that is announced and then falls flat. For example, the challenge could be financial sustainability – either losing money (as in the case study) or not being able to afford to deliver outcomes. Typically, this results in a cost-cutting exercise to decide how costs and budgets can be reduced, but often it delivers no more than half of the promised savings. That lack of outcome has a direct impact on the company.

Secondly, it provides for greater staff and stakeholder engagement. We know that business performance, particularly in the modern world, is highly impacted by how engaged staff and other stakeholders such as customers are. By allowing stakeholders to actively participate you will have a much more engaged and productive organisation that better meets customers' needs.

Thirdly, there will be an audit trail of how the decision was made. Many decisions are subject to scrutiny down track, whether by a national audit office in the public sector or through shareholders in the private sector.

Better decision-making processes, using a rigorous framework that ensures decisions stick, will achieve clarity on how you got to the decision. You will get better staff engagement and will derive better outcomes, which result in improved company and organisational performance.

Better decision making will improve the reputations of organisations and their leaders. You will meet the expectations of the market, shareholders, the public and stakeholders in your organisation; particularly those of the millennial population, whose expectations that they have their say are much higher. Traditional methods of decision making such as 'decide and defend' no longer meet expectations.

Data from Forbes shows that companies that perform better are more sustainable, with more highly engaged employees. An article by Glassdoor also shows that employees who are being paid fairly value additional financial reward less than culture, working conditions and their working environment. Better decision making can support all of these things.

Finally, a company's financial performance is improved when they address outcomes other than financial performance through better decision making. Solely driving decisions to deliver financial outcomes is not the best way to win the financial game.

Jim Collins, author of *Built to Last* and *Good to Great*, noted in an interview with Jerry Useem of *Fortune* magazine that 'it's really the stream of decisions over time, brilliantly executed, that accounts for great outcomes.'

Data from Bloomberg looking at historic financial market data shows that it is more important than ever to deliver non-financial ('intangible') value, as an increasing proportion of the total market capitalisation is based on intangible assets. In a study by Ocean Tomo, you can see that by 2020 over 84% of the value of the S&P 500 companies was from intangible assets.

Why do people think that better decision making is hard?

Making decisions about large, complex problems looks hard because of the different factors at play.

The challenge is to address these head on rather than pretend they don't exist. Let's look at what makes decision making so hard and begin with the world of cognitive bias. There has been much research about the principles of unconscious cognitive bias, in particular Daniel Kahneman's research in his book *Thinking Fast and Slow*. Our brains consist of processes that take control, even when we'd like to think *we* are in control. This book is not a treatise on cognitive bias but there are several factors that are particularly relevant to better decision making:

- **Overconfidence:** the human condition is such that we have greater confidence in our ability to estimate outcomes than we actually have. Therefore, we put greater commitment in our decisions than we should. This can be hard for us to admit to.

- **Availability bias:** our opinions are driven by the information that is available to us. In other words, the world that we live in will have a strong influence over what we believe. On social media, online and digital on demand, often what we believe in comes straight back at us and gets reinforced. This makes it hard for us to challenge our own opinions on decisions.

- **Status quo bias:** as human beings we are driven to stick with what we know. Change is hard for us to embrace. Subsequently, we are biased against making a decision that is going to lead towards change and not maintain the status quo.

In short, as a decision-making tool, the human being is flawed and easily fooled.

Another key reason why decision making can be hard is that large complex decisions involve lots of stakeholders. It may be tempting to say that you don't know many people who are affected by the decision you are making and ignore them, but it is critical to consider the perspectives of everyone who will be impacted. It becomes hard when we think about how to engage them.

In commercial organisations there is a lack of alignment between incentives such as KPIs, salaries or rewards and the outcomes of decisions. Most KPIs measure what you've done, not what you've achieved. That misalignment drives behaviours that are guided by our cognitive bias. We feel we can't measure what we say we care about such as customer satisfaction, organisational culture or staff engagement; therefore, we make decisions to deliver the numbers that we can measure instead. Even tools such as net promoter score (NPS) that allow us to measure customer satisfaction, for instance, can be one-dimensional and miss the richness of what we truly care about.

Data is another major consideration in decision making and the lack of complete, high-quality data is frequently seen as a reason not to make good, structured decisions.

Finally, and by no means exhaustively, the challenge of there being no 'right' answer, or not being able to please all the people all the time, can make it seem too much.

You might think we're doomed and that it's time to close the book. Fortunately, all is not lost. With my years of experience and the many organisations I have impacted in a positive way, I have lots of examples that demonstrate there are ways through.

Gut feeling is no longer enough

As a senior executive, you know your industry and sector well. Your gut is better attuned than anybody else to make decisions. Why not use that? But given all the things we've said about lack of transparency and auditability, just taking your gut feeling or your intuition is no longer enough. There are expectations from the market, stakeholders and the public. You can't stand up in the Royal Commission and say that you invested $1 billion because it felt right.

However, our gut is helpful in decision making but we need to find the balance between making decisions based on intuition versus a purely data-driven and assumption-laden approach. Gut feeling is not something we can put our finger on. Success will only come from a combination of intuition, capability and a rigorous, transparent and better decision-making approach.

One of the opportunities and core concepts of better decision making is shining a light on these two issues. You have to make the implicit (gut feeling) explicit by identifying how you applied that gut feeling.

CASE STUDY – HOW DO WE INVEST TO MAXIMISE IMPACT?

In the investment community, the underlying principle of impact investing is the focus on 'balanced impact', ie non-financial returns, such as environmental benefits and social benefits, alongside financial returns. Commercial property companies like Investa are increasingly exploring the viability of impact investment funds, which are commercial real estate investment vehicles designed to deliver intangible outcomes at the same time as delivering tangible financial returns. Historically, the company used a varied range of tangible and intangible variables such as NABERS (National Australian Built Environment Rating System) ratings, equipment upgrades and capital works records to assess whether the property would deliver enough opportunity to improve the environmental performance (energy consumption, etc) or improve the social outcomes of the public and shared spaces, while delivering market rate returns.

To strengthen this process, Investa decided to build a rigorous decision-making framework that not only drew on the intangible but also enabled them to make defendable decisions cleanly and explicitly on the best property to invest in from an ESG (environmental, social and corporate governance) perspective. They put the P[5] Framework in place, which ultimately attracted large, sophisticated investors into the room during the early ideation phase. The framework ensured they could get clear on what their criteria were and they discussed the objective reasons why one kind of property was a better investment than others. This was articulated explicitly in the framework. They were surprised that the investors indicated they were comfortable making a trade-off between accepting lower financial returns for greater non-financial returns. They did that openly through a better collaborative decision-making process.

This was a real win for Investa because they were able to objectively and transparently balance the environmental, social and financial factors that drive investment decisions. By using the framework, they were able to demonstrate that by universally considering environmental and social factors they could drive returns in those areas most important to impact investors.

Bridging the strategy-execution gap

This is one of the most common challenges for corporations. Expensive facilitators come up with a strategy that the leadership team are proud of and the CEO presents to the board. Everyone sits back and gives two thumbs up. It then becomes an ornament on the CEO's bookshelf while the rest of the organisation gets on with what they've always done – not surprising, given our status quo cognitive bias and the reality that strategy development typically doesn't involve those who will execute it. This situation is also common in public organisations, where 'business as usual' prevails.

Bridging the strategy-execution gap is a decision-making challenge. You will have to decide what to focus on doing and what to stop doing so that you can move resources and reshape the business to deliver your strategy. That will only come with change and decision making. Putting in a better structured decision-making process, particularly around how to execute your strategy, will bridge the strategy-execution gap. Bridging the gap means connecting those at the top of the organisation, who created this strategy, with those at the bottom of the organisation, who are doing the 'doing'. If you build that bridge through better decision-making processes, engaging people up and down the organisation, you will be able to execute your strategy. The bottom of the organisation will start to make decisions about what they should be doing, guided by the strategy. Suddenly, the whole organisation gets lined up on delivering the strategy.

Governance is not decision making

Strong governance frameworks do not enable us to make better decisions. Governance ensures that the organisation is doing what it says it does; for example, that the board of directors represents the shareholders appropriately or that a Cabinet committee ensures a government department fulfils its role properly. Governance bodies should participate in decision-making processes.

Governance gives us confidence that our decisions are consistent and valid but it is not the job of governance teams to decide what decision should be made. That is the role of the organisations' decision-makers. Being upfront about this will mean greater clarity when we look at how different parts of the organisation may participate in better decision-making processes.

JANE'S IT PROJECT PORTFOLIO CHALLENGE

Jane was struggling with a long list of IT projects. She didn't have enough resource in her team to execute all of the projects and was constantly being given new IT project requests from different medical practitioners and other parts of the business – new anaesthetic information systems, new computed tomography (CT) imaging systems, new asset management systems, etc.

Jane wanted to be able to understand the overall priorities across the whole hospital, including her own IT team's priorities, so she could decide which of all the projects she should execute and which she should delay or not do at all. She wanted the support of the whole health board so the decisions would stick.

Before starting to address her IT project portfolio challenge, Jane assumed that her IT governance board would make the decisions about which projects to deliver and which to defer. She soon realised that, while the governance board might have the final sign-off, their role as a governance body was to endorse or validate the decisions brought to them – but not to actually make the decisions. Certainly, many of the individual members of the governance board would be involved as stakeholders in any decision process, but not strictly in their governance capacity. Making a distinction between these two different contexts for stakeholder participation was an important first step for Jane.

Avoiding pitfalls

Here are some common pitfalls when thinking about organisational decision making:

- **Dismissing gut feeling in decision making:** in our modern, data-driven world it's very tempting to treat gut feel as inappropriate, or even dangerous, in decision making. However, bringing experience, knowledge and other context to bear on decisions is critical, it just needs to be done in a conscious, structured way.

- **Assuming the strategy is a decision-making tool:** your strategy may well have been intentionally created as a tool to support decision making throughout the organisation, but many strategies have not. There needs to be an explicit connection between the strategy and the decisions that drive the day-to-day business, and this is frequently missing.

- **Treating governance arrangements as the only way of making complex decisions:** the creative work of decision making should happen outside of governance processes, or at least should be undertaken as an activity that stakeholders in governance bodies participate in completely separate from their formal governance, compliance and risk-management responsibilities.

Reflection

Think about decision making in your organisation today and reflect on the following questions:

1. Does your decision making feel 'typical'? For example, do decisions often not stick and frequently not get actioned? Do decisions get over-turned later, once scrutinised?

2. Do you see cognitive bias at play in your decision making – both looking at yourself and your colleagues?

3. Does your organisation live by your strategy and is your strategy used as a tool to support decision making?

Summary

Better decision making or Decision Thinking is conscious, structured, has stakeholders participate, better delivers on organisational outcomes and has greater rigour and clarity. We care about that because our reputations and money are at stake. Businesses and organisations care about delivering outcomes. If that's important to you, better decision making is essential.

Better decision making seems hard because there are so many challenges that seem impossible to solve. That makes the traditional ways of decision making – decide and defend, or purely data-driven approaches – stay in place.

Gut feeling is an important part of better decision making, but how do we make the best use of it? Make it explicit along with all the other aspects of the decision so that we give everyone (and everything) a chance to do what they do best.

If we can address large complex decisions well, we can bridge the strategy-execution gap. We can make better investment decisions and we can set our organisations up for success. Once we start to talk about how different parts of the organisation can fit together in decision making, it becomes clear that saying that we have governance does not mean we have better decision making.

In Chapter 2 we will look in depth at the four core principles of the P^5 Decision Framework, which we have developed to aid organisations make more effective decisions.

2
The P⁵ Decision Framework

Underlying principles

It's all very well to talk about better decision making, but what do we mean by that? Decision Thinking is transparent, clear and consistent, delivers on all the outcomes required and ultimately gives us decisions that stick. But how do we do it? Frankly, if you're reading this book and you're not interested in that, I suggest you put it down and go and invest in a new coin to toss to make your decisions. In this chapter we will discuss the core principles that form the basis of the P⁵ Decision Framework and take you through an overview of the framework's five phases.

There is a huge body of science around decision making. A lot of people don't know this. We all know of maths, physics and chemistry, but decision science is a science discipline in itself; it looks at how decisions are made, the theoretical underpinning to all decisions, otherwise known as decision theory. Like many other branches of science, the challenge is in the practical application of it. Good theory, but how do you make it work in the real world?

My Catalyze colleagues, other practitioners and I have spent decades putting decision theory into practice in Australia, the UK and New Zealand and across the globe. This book is my distillation of that experience – how to put the theory into practice in a way that works. In doing this, I've distinguished four principles that underpin the P^5 Decision Framework.

Let's cover the principles briefly first as these are foundational to the entire framework:

1. **Process before content:** separate out 'how' the decision is made and agree this first before you start work on the content ('what' the decision is).

2. **Academic rigour:** base your process on proven decision science and understand the limitations of methods used and the impact of assumptions.

3. **Active stakeholder participation:** engage stakeholders widely. Encourage them to participate actively in meaningful ways in the decision process, not just in traditional

consultation, with regular agreement and commitment as the process proceeds.

4. **Intangible and tangible value:** take all forms of value, intangible, financial, non-financial, and tangible, into account in decision making.

An overarching theme of the principles is the idea of making the implicit explicit. This means using a clear process, having explicit involvement of stakeholders and their perspectives, explicit use of rigorous decision-making decision theory and explicit consideration of the intangible (or implicit) value.

None of this is rocket science. What these principles support, and what Decision Thinking does, is making explicit what's actually going on with most decision making every day. We don't normally realise it, or sometimes don't want to admit it.

One of the ways we see this at play is in the principle of buyer's remorse. That brand new car you were so excited to buy turns out to be not as great as you thought. You don't like it once you get it home. Our unconscious decision process, driven by things like cognitive bias, such as thinking, 'All my mates have one so I've got to get one,' has not actually considered what's really important to us. We've made a purchasing decision without explicitly considering what we really care about. When we live with it, it really isn't what we wanted.

Why do I believe these four principles underpin better decision making? Let's look at each in more depth.

Process before content

Let's get clear on the difference between how the decision is made and the decision content (*what* we are deciding). Usually in decision making it is the content that is contentious: 'My proposal is more important than yours', 'My investment is better than yours' or 'My idea is smarter than yours'. That's all about the content, the idea, the proposal or the investment.

If we define and agree the process before we get anywhere near the content, we can start from a place of agreement, not conflict. Generally, people are happy to agree the process by which they'll reach a decision. That's because they are not saying what the decision outcome will be in the beginning so they don't need to deal with the contentious issues early on. Once the process is agreed, and especially if that gains the buy-in and commitment of senior leaders or stakeholders, then decisions are much less likely to be re-contested down track. Conversely, without that explicit agreed process, it's easy for leaders or other stakeholders later not to agree with the decision and contest or overturn it, saying they wouldn't have made it that way.

We can also use a decision model as a helpful way of representing our decision content within a process.

The process becomes about building and then evaluating that model, not arguing about content. We all know the maxim that 'all models are wrong and some are useful'. The trick is to build a useful model, intended to make the parts of the process and the decision explicit so that everyone can get on the same page well before facing the hard question of the decision itself. This principle is about doing the work to get as much agreement and alignment around process and models before you get stuck into whether you should do X or Y.

An excellent example of this principle is when the New Zealand Defence Force (NZDF) had a major decision to make, which I'll come back to later in this chapter. They got the decision-making process signed off by the ultimate stakeholders – the joint Ministers of Defence and Finance – who needed to make the final decision. With that sign-off achieved before the process even began, everyone involved could be confident that once the process was complete and a recommendation was made, it would receive a good hearing at the highest levels of government.

Following this work, the Minister of Defence at the time, Dr Jonathan Coleman, in his speech to the Defence Industry Association annual conference, said: 'The process [the Catalyze P⁵ Decision Framework] was robust, analytically sound, and data-driven. It has been identified as an exemplar for other government departments to follow.'

Academic rigour

If we build our decision process on a foundation of academic rigour, such as decision science, we can have much greater confidence in the outcome and make the decisions more resilient to scrutiny because of the strength of the theoretical underpinnings. There is a vast body of work in the field of decision science; this is not intended to be an academic text so I will only scratch the surface here.

At the simplest level, decision theory tells us that coherent decisions are based on the value associated with the consequences of the decision and the probability of realising those consequences. You need to maximise what we call the 'overall expected value', but determining what value will be realised and the probability of realising it isn't easy. This is because decisions are about the future and we therefore need to make some subjective judgements. Unfortunately, until Tesla launches a time machine, we can't predict the future.

Decision science helps us here if used in an appropriate and practical way. It provides methods by which we can discuss and represent value, in much the same way as you might represent other properties in the real world, such as using the Celsius or Fahrenheit scale to represent temperature. Typically, this way of thinking about decision making is known as value-focused thinking, concentrating on the value something delivers, such as environmental sustainability, staff satisfaction or customer satisfaction. This is the 'why' of a decision, as opposed to the thing that is delivered, such as a more energy-efficient building or a new car – the 'what' of a decision. Distinguishing the 'what' from the 'why' is helpful in decision making.

Active stakeholder participation

My experience suggests that re-contesting or lack of execution of a decision or decisions that don't stick often come from disenfranchised stakeholders, which could include staff, board members, politicians or the public, who exert their influence after the decision has been made. It's much better to take them on the journey of the decision; their input is invaluable. That's easier said than done.

The key is to find clear, practical ways of engaging stakeholders, not just as a token gesture. You might, for example, work with stakeholders to create the process, develop decision options or sign off the process. As you'll see when we look at the P⁵ Framework, there are many points where stakeholders can participate actively, not just in 'consultation'.

It's also important to ask stakeholders how they'd like to participate. It's easy to make assumptions but you can't beat finding out from stakeholders how they would like to be engaged in the decision. People are much more likely to accept a decision that didn't go their way if they can see clearly how it was made and also how their views and perspectives were taken into account, even if they didn't agree with the outcome. The decision is ultimately going to get made and it can't possibly go the way that everyone wants it to go when you've got a diverse range of stakeholders and limited resources. Somehow, we have to get the support and commitment to the decision of those stakeholders who didn't get their way.

In Chapter 1 I described the commercial real estate case study, which is a perfect example of active stakeholder participation. Investors weren't just consulted, they actively participated in a hands-on workshop where they explored and agreed the trade-offs between the financial and the non-financial (environmental and social) outcomes. It was an interactive process, not just a consultation, and the work that was done in that workshop was then carried forward in the rest of the P^5 Framework. Investors are not usually invited 'into the tent' when designing the investment criteria of a fund, so this was a market-leading first, which resulted in a co-created model that really delivered on the intent of an impact investment fund.

Intangible and tangible value

Decisions often don't deliver the outcomes required and the evidence suggests that's because of an over-focus on tangible value, which most often means dollars, profit and revenue. Many people think it's too hard to consider intangible value, which by definition is hard to measure. It's easier to ignore it and pretend it doesn't matter – but just because it can't be measured using traditional methods does not mean it is unimportant. All of those intangible outcomes that we don't take into account in our decision making but come back to bite us later are another source of buyers' remorse.

If we look back at decision theory, we *can* consider the intangible value in our decisions if we can articulate it clearly and find a valid way to represent it. Obviously, we can consider things like temperature once we have a scale to represent it, eg Celsius or Fahrenheit. This doesn't mean reducing every aspect of value to a lowest common denominator, such as dollars. You should treat value in a way that more accurately reflects the nature of that value itself. If we are to avoid buyers' remorse or, much worse, organisational failure from poor decisions, we need to explicitly (there's that word again) consider all aspects of value in our decision making.

In the previous chapter, we talked about the UK company who turned their business around from negative growth to putting a lot of money on their bottom line. Initially, their decision making only took into account revenue and profit, which was one of the reasons they were going backwards. Once they started to put the structured decision framework in place, it became clear that what they actually cared about was innovation, customer satisfaction and staff satisfaction, as well as revenue and profit. Once they considered all those things explicitly and could choose to trade them off against the financial numbers, they ended up with better financial performance as well.

Core components of the P⁵ Decision Framework

The four underlying principles sound good in theory but how do we implement them into the five phases in the P⁵ Framework? In the chapters that follow, we will explore each phase in greater detail, covering the core foundations of each phase, what it can look like in real life, and we'll look at a case study relevant to each one. We'll also cover the keys to success and what to watch for. In this chapter I give you an overview of each phase:

1. **Plan:** this is where you get clear on the decision you are making, who should be involved in making it and what the timeline and key dates are. You develop a clear plan, then you agree and sign off the plan.

2. **Prepare:** there are two parts to this phase. Part 1 covers what you value; what matters to you and your stakeholders. Here you deal with this

tangible and intangible consideration. In Part 2 you look at the alternatives you have, what your options might be, your choices, investments and projects. By the end of the Prepare phase you will be clear on and have agreed what you value and what your alternatives are.

3. **Prioritise:** you will find out how these alternative options deliver value when compared to each other. You identify the order of priority of your alternatives so that everything is lined up and compare them so you can see which option is better than another.

4. **Package:** you turn those priorities into real options such as an implementation plan for the organisation. In this phase, you find out what you will invest in and do, and also what you won't. This shows what decision you need to make.

5. **Present:** now you are ready to present to the ultimate authority, perhaps the board or the Cabinet.

Key to this framework is that between each of the phases there is an explicit agreement step: do the stakeholders agree to the process, the options, the criteria, the prioritisation, the package and the decision?

The diagram below shows the P⁵ Decision Framework and the four Decision Thinking principles.

Figure 2.1: The P⁵ Decision Framework, built on the four principles of Decision Thinking

JANE'S IT PROJECT PORTFOLIO CHALLENGE

With the help of experts in Decision Thinking, Jane designed a transparent, collaborative decision process, based on the P⁵ Framework. She designed the process before considering any of the IT proposals (process before content), she decided to use multi-criteria decision analysis (MCDA) for prioritising proposals (academic rigour), she brought various stakeholders in to help design the process (active stakeholder participation) and she ensured all aspects of value, both clinical and business, were included in the consideration of proposals (intangible and tangible value).

CASE STUDY – HOW DO WE CREATE A SUSTAINABLE DEFENCE FORCE?

The NZDF faced a challenge of long-term financial sustainability and the government asked them to do what was called at the time a defence midpoint rebalancing review (DMRR). They had already run the usual savings and efficiency measures and completed several spending reviews. But these hadn't yielded what they had promised. In fact, NZDF had achieved significantly less savings than they thought they might get from those initiatives. The NZDF and the Ministry of Defence needed something more drastic. They needed a process that would support their fundamental decision: what was the best possible, affordable Defence Force? We helped them put a structured decision-making process into place based on the P⁵ Decision Framework. Let's cover what happened in each phase in turn.

1. **Plan:** in this phase Defence set up a project team and agreed the timing for the review and who the stakeholders should be. They looked across the whole of government, even outside of NZDF, and put governance arrangements in place to agree the process. They agreed who had the ownership and who the sponsors were. It was important to get these key issues nailed down because this allowed senior stakeholders, including ministers, to agree the process. Everyone who participated could be confident that whatever recommendations came

out had the best chance of getting implemented following formal Cabinet decision making.

2. **Prepare:** in Part 1 of this phase the project team ran a series of workshops with senior stakeholders to agree why New Zealand has a Defence Force and how the NZDF provides value to stakeholders. The results of that were also signed off by the ultimate sponsors, the joint Ministers of Finance and Defence. In Part 2 of the Prepare phase, a decision was reached to use a zero-based approach. This is the principle of imagining a future where you can buy, build, invest in and construct the most desirable Defence Force of the future, starting from the 'ground up'. This gave Defence an opportunity to look at the impact of making changes in particular areas and how this might affect other parts of Defence. This is a creative and positive way of exploring options for cost saving or changing where investments are made.

3. **Prioritise:** NZDF built a decision model based on MCDA, which we'll discuss in a later chapter. They used a group of senior stakeholders to assess how the alternatives for defence would deliver value, and then they prioritised on value for money, so that they could work out what was the best bang for the buck.

4. **Package:** NZDF took that hypothetical order of priority and developed it into realistic and affordable package options for the future of defence. This was the chance for them to consider the military coherence, financial sustainability, affordability and 'doability' of each option.

5. **Present:** here Defence took the recommended packages from the Package phase and turned them

into the standard Cabinet documentation required by the government to make a decision.

The result of NZDF running a structured decision-making process based on the P^5 Framework for the DMRR was a satisfied government, which made a decision swiftly and agreed, rather than cutting defence funding back or funding at current levels, to invest further in defence because ministers were clear on the value and the risks and opportunity costs of cutting back. This resulted in over $500 million of additional funding for the NZDF and an award from the Minister of Defence for Catalyze.

Since this decision was made, NZDF and the Ministry of Defence have continued to use the DMRR decision model as a reference point for subsequent funding and for performance improvement framework reviews.

Avoiding pitfalls

Here are some areas to keep an eye on when embarking on putting structured decision making into place:

- **Treating it like a 'recipe':** the P^5 Framework is intended as a framework to guide the development of decision process to suit a very wide range of decision-making situations, so expect to design, customise and configure appropriate process to suit your specific situation.

- **Ignoring the principles or picking and choosing between them:** it can be tempting to override or shortcut the principles ('we don't have time to engage stakeholders', for example) but this will invariably lead back to poor decision making and not deliver on what's possible: complex decisions made easy, that stick.

- **Confusing something else with structured decision making:** most organisations have many tools, processes, policies and programmes in place for delivering change, project management, financial management, etc. These may all be context for, or an input to, structured decision making, but they are in place for a specific, different purpose.

Reflection

Think about your current approach to complex decision making and consider whether each of the four principles is in place:

1. Do you have a clear, documented, agreed process to follow for complex decisions?

2. Is there sound theory behind any evaluation models or tools you use?

3. How are stakeholders involved in your major decisions (if at all)?

4. How is value (both financial and non-financial) considered in your complex decisions?

Summary

It is possible to put better decision making in place with greater transparency and consistency. Experience shows that building a phased decision process founded on the Decision Thinking principles makes all the difference.

As a reminder, these are the four principles of Decision Thinking:

1. **Process before content:** this includes using things such as decision models.

2. **Academic rigour:** this involves basing our decision process on decision science and the ideas of value-focused thinking.

3. **Active stakeholder participation:** look through the process and see how key stakeholders can participate in meaningful ways.

4. **Tangible and intangible value:** find a way to represent intangible value on a level playing field.

At its heart, better decision making is all about making the implicit explicit and getting everything on the table so stakeholders can grapple with it.

Over the next few chapters, we will look at each phase of the P^5 Decision Framework. In Chapter 3 we will start with Plan and look in detail at the importance of the planning phase to the success of the decision-making process.

3
Plan

Setting up for success

Everyone knows the maxim, 'Perfect preparation prevents poor performance.' Stephen Covey says in *The 7 Habits of Highly Effective People*, 'Let's begin with the end in mind.' That's the principle of the Plan phase.

The problem or challenge or opportunity we're looking at might not feel like a decision-making challenge. It might feel like a business or a strategy problem. Often, what people are dealing with is not 'I've got a complex decision to make'. It's more often a problem that, only through discovery and conversation, turns into a difficult decision that needs to be made, which will make a difference in the organisation. For example, you might think, 'I haven't got enough budget for the future to fund my department/my division/my business unit.' That's not a decision, it's a problem. Following some exploration, the underlying decision might be: 'I've got to decide how to save money.' Or, more specifically, 'I've got to decide which activities I should stop doing that will save me money and which activities I should focus on doing to achieve our objectives affordably.' Then it becomes a decision on what you should or should not do to save money.

Here are some examples of typical problems and the decisions that may be underneath those problems:

Problem/challenge/ opportunity	Decision
Too many projects to execute	What projects to approve and which to reject?
Organisation not delivering the strategy	Which strategic initiatives will deliver the vision and which won't?
Company staff not aligned and pulling together	Which activities are aligned with company and staff values and which aren't?
Not achieving required growth	Which products or markets to exit and which ones to focus on or enter?
How to deliver 'value for money' from the public purse	Which investments will deliver the best 'bang for buck' for the public and which will deliver the least?

Framing a problem as a decision is an important part of the Plan phase. This is why we use the term Decision Thinking; once we start thinking consciously about the decisions needing to be made, we're on our way to solving our problems or embracing our opportunities. If we can't identify the decision that needs to be made, a better decision process won't help us.

There are many different shapes of problem that the P⁵ Framework can address. In this book I will focus on what I call 'portfolio-type' decisions but this framework applies regardless of the type of decision you are making. This is where you have a range of options (such as projects to execute) and you've got to pick the best set out of them, rather than picking the best single alternative from a set. My academic colleagues call this the 'knapsack problem' – you are going on a hike and have a fixed size and capacity backpack and need to decide the optimum combination of items to carry that fit in the backpack and will give the most value on your hike.

Many organisations are now using the discipline of 'portfolio management', and one of the most common methodologies is the Axelos (formerly the UK Government) 'Management of Portfolios' (MoP) approach. In such disciplines there is often a view of two cycles that work in tandem – **define** the portfolio and **manage** the portfolio. The P⁵ Framework is a natural approach to support portfolio definition.

Questions to ask in the Plan phase

As we go through each phase, I'll give you a list of questions that might help you get set up for success. The questions you might want to ask during this phase are:

1. What is the problem I need to address or opportunity I want to take?

2. Who is the ultimate sponsor who will sign off the solution?

3. When does it need solving by? It's essential that the design and execution of the P^5 Framework fit within the 'real-world' timeframes of the organisation.

4. What else is going on in my organisation that this problem might need to make an impact on (for example, setting budgets, hiring staff or quarterly objectives)?

5. What decision would I need to take to solve it? Decision making is critical to making a difference. If there are no decisions, there will be no change. If there's no change, nothing will move forward.

6. What type of decision is it? Is it an investment decision, resource allocation decision, a decision to pivot your business or a decision to exit something?

7. How does it fit within the 'business as usual' processes (for example, the authorisation of budgets and sign-off of head count)?

8. Who is impacted by the decision? Get clear on who your stakeholders are and categorise them by type and how they are impacted.

9. How will those stakeholders participate?

10. What other contexts are relevant? Our current situation? Budgets, financial constraints, forecasts or strategy? This includes what previous decisions may be off the table or what other commitments have already been made.

11. Who is going to run the decision process and how do we resource it with time and effort?

12. What are the governance arrangements around the decision (such as sign-off authorities)? Remember, governance is not decision making but it has a role to play.

The end game is to build a clear plan that covers all five phases in the P^5 Framework. The next critical step is to get this agreed by the ultimate sponsor, who will sign off on the final decision that impacts the problem. Every phase in the P^5 Framework has a distinct 'agree' point, which is critical. This will ensure we have stakeholders on board throughout the decision process; every time we come to an agree point, if there are people who aren't aligned, we have an opportunity to correct that.

This is a good point to introduce one of the watch words of structured decision making: *requisite*. This means that something is required or necessary for a particular purpose or decision. I think of *requisite* as 'sufficient to solve the problem'. The job in the Plan phase is to get clear on what is requisite. If the decision is a one- or two-million-dollar investment that impacts a small group of stakeholders, we don't need five phases that are going to take a year to execute on. Equally, if the decision changes the entire direction of a 10,000-person organisation, then trying to do it in two weeks will not be requisite. We'll ask this throughout the rest of the book. What is requisite? What is sufficient to solve the problem?

Before we move on to the foundations of the Plan phase, let's get clear on the important issue of stakeholders.

Stakeholders

We often get confused between stakeholders *in* the decision (the people who might have to take the decision) and stakeholders *of* the decision (people who benefit from or are impacted by the results of the decision). For example, the chief financial officer (CFO) is typically a stakeholder in the decision because he or she is going to sign off on the financial implications. But the implications of the decision will impact much more widely. The CFO might be a stakeholder for signing off on the budget but a budget might lead to some change that impacts a large group of staff, which then impacts the customers. Consequently, staff and customers may well be stakeholders of the decision.

We've got to look at the stakeholders in the decision process and the stakeholders of the result of the decision made, because it is essential to include the right stakeholders in the decision-making process. Think broadly first and then narrow down to those who will be directly impacted by the decision. For example, working with the Australian Department of Finance across the whole of the Australian Federal Government, we know that the Australian people are stakeholders. But even though Australia exports to China and the Chinese people are impacted by what the Australian government does, we may not consider China as a stakeholder of a decision to allocate Australian government funding.

In a single government department, for example the Australian Department of Defence, we would consider which stakeholders to involve, depending on the decision. If the decision is about the entire Defence Force, again, the Australian public would be a stakeholder. But if the decision is about the best kind of aircraft to acquire, we would include the Royal Australian Air Force and other agencies that use Air Force resources plus defence industry companies as potential suppliers, but we would not include the Australian public. The key question is: what is the requisite range of stakeholders?

Flexibility is important as there may be stakeholders you are not aware of at first who will need to be brought into the process once discovered. Sometimes there is a strong temptation to avoid including some stakeholders; for example, in a decision with significant environmental impacts, global environmental lobby groups might be stakeholders. They may well have firm views so it might seem easier to exclude them, but I would always encourage their inclusion right from the start to avoid any possibility that a stakeholder might have the influence to overturn decisions made. Remember that active and meaningful stakeholder participation is one of the principles of the P^5 Framework and key to its success.

Foundations of the Plan phase

Each of the P^5 phases is grounded in specific foundations, including our four 'core' principles. For the Plan phase the key foundations are as follows:

1. **Context is decisive:** the first piece of context is the 'problem statement' – what are we trying to solve or achieve? Context is also the current environment; for example, there could be a general election imminent and therefore an impetus to make decisions. Context may also be the future environment or the history. Understanding context is crucial as we could easily tackle the wrong decision and design our

framework in a way that doesn't help us go in the right direction in an appropriate amount of time.

2. **Process before content:** separate the decision process from the decision content. Focus on the process we will execute to reach the decision, not what the right decision is.

3. **Active and diverse stakeholder participation:** in the Plan phase we look at how stakeholders could participate. Diversity is the power in decision making. Cloverpop, in their report of September 2017, showed that better decisions were made 80% of the time when a group of people were brought together from diverse age ranges, genders and locations.

How does all of this work in practice? The following case study lists the ways one company used the Plan phase of the P⁵ Framework to successfully set up their decision-making process.

CASE STUDY – HOW BEST TO DECOMMISSION OIL AND GAS INFRASTRUCTURE?

We worked with a major oil and gas company based in Western Australia who needed to make a critical decision on decommissioning sub-sea oil and gas infrastructure. As an organisation they were committed to stakeholder participation and transparent decision making. They decided to use a structured decision-making process known as 'comparative assessment', designed from the P⁵ Decision Framework.

They took the time to design the process before making decisions. In the oil and gas industry, stakeholders are diverse, ranging from the recreational fisher to large organisations and government departments. They decided how stakeholders could participate by asking them.

They then looked ahead to the Prioritisation phase and planned a two-stage approach. The first step was to involve only internal stakeholders, as discussions would be highly technical, and then use external stakeholders to validate the work of this internal group and add their own perspectives on the non-technical (environmental, social, etc) aspects of the decision.

These steps proved to be effective, with some great participation and positive feedback received and clear alignment on the way forward.

Planning in practice

The Plan phase starts with a discovery process to find out important context. The starting context may include the organisation's purpose, strategy, business plans and other core documents. The Plan phase might then include a workshop with senior stakeholders to explore what the problem is and what could help solve this – in particular, the decisions we might need to make. We consider objectives for the decision – what are we trying to achieve? We look at potential constraints and the underlying assumptions we've made. Testing those constraints and assumptions is crucial and connects with the approach of making the implicit explicit. In the Prepare phase, we'll discuss criteria – frequently criteria and constraints are confused. Criteria help you choose between different alternatives. Constraints filter out alternatives and are hard limits we can't break.

We then look at stakeholders – senior leadership, the board, ministers, other agencies or departments – and how they will participate. You might include the global vice president, customers and staff. In Prepare, stakeholders could contribute ideas through a workshop. In the Prioritise phase, they could evaluate and prioritise options against criteria. They can help turn these priorities into real decision options in the Package phase and they may contribute to briefing presentations to senior leaders in the Present phase.

The Plan phase includes key design decisions about each of the later phases. For example, you might consider taking a 'zero-based' approach. This approach can contribute hugely to the success of a significant decision. If your problem is the financial sustainability of your department or organisation, you have to make decisions on what to stop and what to focus on doing. Most stakeholders are happy to discuss what to add but not what to give up. Taking a zero-based approach means that you imagine you have nothing at all. Instead of looking at how to save 10%, you'll look at how to build an organisation from 'nothing' that costs 90% of what it costs today. This approach is not for the faint-hearted because you have to look at your entire organisation, but it can be critical to solving big problems. That key decision during the Plan phase impacts on the Prepare phase.

For Prioritise, we make decisions during Plan on the methodology for prioritisation and decide who to involve in that process, and how.

For the Package phase, we decide during Plan on the scenarios or different future environments we want to test our decision against.

Finally, for the Present phase, we need to decide where the output from Package is going to go and who needs to see it. Do we need to write a Cabinet paper or a board paper? What needs to be wrapped around the outputs from our decision process?

The last piece of the Plan phase is the agreement to the Plan – a common feature between each of the phases of the P^5 Framework. This is a great opportunity to have stakeholders engaged and aligned with the way the decision will be made and is essential to set up for success.

JANE'S IT PROJECT PORTFOLIO CHALLENGE

In Jane's case, she had the Plan signed off by the IT governance board, which comprised a number of senior representatives from both the clinical side of the health board and the administrative side – including the chief operating officer, the chief financial officer and the chief medical officer. Jane consulted and engaged stakeholders across the health board in the planning process and agreed the key steps, dates, numbers of workshops, etc.

CASE STUDY – HOW DO WE ACHIEVE LONG-TERM SUSTAINABILITY FOR A SECTOR?

This case study will illustrate how a sector of the New Zealand government made up of three key agencies used a structured decision process developed from the P^5 Framework to address fundamental strategic issues raised by the government.

During the Plan phase, they set up a cross-government governance group of senior stakeholders to agree the arrangements for signing off the key steps of each phase. Their first task was to sign off the Plan phase. The process was designed by lead representatives from the three agencies involved, who ensured the leaders in those organisations were briefed and engaged in the discussions. Through those briefings, they refined the process design.

The plan was then taken to the governance group and, following their input, they signed off the plan. An internal project team was also set up, which included a senior leader seconded from each of the three agencies, with the ability to commit resources and participants from their own organisations. This meant that there was clear time and effort available to execute the decision process.

One of their key principles was to start this decision process as they meant to proceed, thereby engaging stakeholders immediately in the Plan phase. This was the first time these three agencies had ever collaborated on a shared outcome of this strategic significance. It was a milestone for them to come together and agree the outcomes of the Plan phase, and this led to effective execution of the rest of the framework and ultimately strong support from government for the recommendations. As a result of this process, the agencies received a significant (tens of millions of dollars) funding boost from government.

Avoiding pitfalls

Having got the scars, I'd rather you didn't get them as well. This list of pitfalls is by no means exhaustive but will give you a flavour of what to look out for:

- **Answering the wrong question:** not allowing sufficient time, deliberation and discovery of the real problem and the decisions that need to be made can lead to a process that doesn't achieve what's needed.

- **A false timeline:** you may feel you have to make a decision by a particular time but, frequently, those timelines aren't what matters. Test and challenge that in the Plan phase. While we want requisite process, we equally want a process that isn't overly constrained and hurried.

- **Intentional exclusion of stakeholders:** some people say they don't want to involve them because they will disrupt the process and never agree, but that's contrary to the whole point of active stakeholder participation.

- **Not looking widely enough to find stakeholders:** as well as mixing up stakeholders in the decision process versus stakeholders of the decision outcome. Remember, diversity improves decision effectiveness. Look widely and always be prepared to go further.

- **Not setting aside sufficient time and resource to run the process:** it takes time and effort to bring people together. If they don't have the time to put in, it will result in failure or require additional expenditure to put things right later.

- **Overkill or underkill:** some people run a six-month process for a decision that doesn't impact many people and doesn't have a major outcome or, conversely, try to do it in a much shorter of period of time than is required. Or they might spend too much time on the things that are concrete and measurable and too little time on the issues that are less well known.

- **Thinking that the Plan phase is about making the decision:** people start saying that they know the right answer and get diverted into discussion around the decision itself.

- **Constraints that aren't constraints:** uncover what constraints really are and not just what others think are important issues in the decision process.

These are a few things to watch out for that can make a big difference to the set-up of the decision process. The biggest pitfall is rushing the Plan phase and jumping straight into the process. The time 'saved' by rushing the Plan phase is lost multiple times over in subsequent phases.

Reflection

1. Make a list of who you would consider key stakeholders in the big decisions you make and divide it into stakeholders in the decision process and stakeholders of the decision outcome. This will give you a useful place to start if you run a Plan phase.

2. Take the table of problems and the underlying decisions and add your own thoughts to that. Take time to ask: 'What's the decision that, if made, would solve this problem?' If you start to look at your problem through a decision 'lens', it may well give you some insight into how to move forward.

Summary

The Plan phase is about beginning with the end in mind and getting clear on the decision we're trying to make. What's the problem and, therefore, what's the decision? Be clear on the who, what, how, when and where of the decision process at a requisite level of detail, which might include dates for workshops, venues, participant lists, or it might be at a higher level.

We've covered the key aspects of what planning involves, including different ways stakeholders can participate, and we pointed to using a hypothetical zero-based approach as an opportunity for solving really big challenges.

In short, starting with a clear, considered and agreed plan will have us set up for decision success.

In Chapter 4 we will discuss the first part of the Prepare phase, where we will look at what is important about the decision we are making and its tangible and intangible value to the organisation. In Chapter 5 we consider what our alternatives in the decision might be. It's common for these two parts to run concurrently, with one informing the other and vice versa.

4
Prepare Value

What is value?

We talk about value-focused thinking and how we naturally make decisions based on value. But what is value? I think of value as everything that we and stakeholders care about, which may seem a strange concept in the world of business and in a business book. In decision making, value includes aspects we care about that will impact upon the decision. Typically, these only get articulated in financial terms. In a corporation, there may well be profit, revenue, or profit growth or revenue growth, all coming down to dollars.

As human beings and as organisations, not-for-profits, corporations and government departments, we care about much more than just financial outcomes. Customer satisfaction, social and environmental outcomes, staff engagement, reputation and quality are also important issues. To make rigorous, transparent and successful decisions, our job needs to be to understand and make explicit how the results of our decision provide value. In the world of decision making and decision science, aspects of value are defined in several ways, with one particularly important representation being criteria.

My job in this book is to make explicit what we mean by criteria as an essential part of a better decision-making framework. As the scope of this book is focused on portfolio decisions, that is, picking many alternatives from many, our main goal is to get the best overall value for a given level of resource or investment (or some other constraint), which we call value for money.

The first part of the Prepare phase is about creating a clear, commonly held basis for articulating value and therefore expected value from a decision outcome. If we get this phase right then most of the struggle in making complex decisions will go away. When we scratched the surface of decision theory in the previous chapter, we noted that the best decisions are made by maximising the outcome of our decision. By that we mean maximising value. Decision theory often talks about decision modelling as a way of comparing things using a common metric of value. We talk a lot about non-financial value in this book, as one of our four fundamental principles is considering both the intangible and tangible value.

Value is more than just money

Why not just care about profit or revenue or the money? Laurence Fink, one of the great investors of today and the CEO of BlackRock, which has over $6 trillion worth of funds under management, shared a draft of a letter to business leaders with Andrew Ross Sorkin from the *New York Times*. Sorkin quotes Fink's letter: 'To prosper over time, every company must not only deliver financial performance, but also show how it makes a positive contribution to society.' The letter caused huge ripples throughout Wall Street and the global financial community because Black-Rock, a financially focused organisation, made it clear that their future vision for successful organisations is based on delivering intangible value as well as tangible value. It also meets stakeholder expectations and staff expectations by addressing non-financial outcomes. We build organisations that are better places to work, that make a difference, and that, as Fink says, make a positive contribution to society.

Fink is not a lone voice – in 2019, in Washington, the Business Roundtable redefined the purpose of a corporation by updating their statement, signed by 181 CEOs who committed to leading their companies for the benefit of all stakeholders – customers, employees, suppliers, communities and shareholders. Reflecting on the new statement, Darren Walker, President of the Ford Foundation, noted:

> 'This is tremendous news because it is more critical than ever that businesses in the 21st century are focused on generating long-term value for all stakeholders and addressing the challenges we face, which will result in shared prosperity and sustainability for both business and society.'

This is important to all of us, even though we don't know how to incorporate non-financial value in our decision making. Typically, intangible outcomes are ignored because they are too hard to articulate. If someone asks you what you care about, often it is the tangible things that come to mind, such as a financially stable future for your family, and the challenge is to identify the intangible value that matters to you.

We need a rigorous decision process that deals with value in its native form and not just by saying that everything we care about has a dollar number. Current generations coming into the workplace are just as interested in purpose, working environment and organisational culture as they are in receiving higher salaries. Organisations will perform better overall by focusing on purpose as well as profit and will be more sustainable places to work because people will be fully engaged and productive. Looking at non-financial value as well as financial value delivers better results, better organisations, better corporations and better government departments and services.

Questions to ask in the Prepare Value phase

1. What makes one alternative more attractive than another?

2. What do we and our stakeholders value?

3. What does 'good' look like in the outcome of a decision? What about 'bad'? When we think of a decision as 'good', what do we mean by that? Why is it a 'good' (or 'bad') decision?

4. What are the trade-offs we might need to make in making this decision?

The second part of the Prepare phase is about defining alternatives, which we will detail later. We often work these two parts iteratively in parallel as the conversations and thinking can happen at the same time. Sometimes we'll make reference to the work we're doing, for example, in Prepare Alternatives to help us identify things that we value. But in Prepare Value we find ways to articulate the intangible things we care about in order to compare alternatives.

Start by looking at things that you intuitively think of as attractive and identify the alternatives that feel appealing to you. Consider what it is that makes them attractive, comparing one to another. For example, when we buy a car, we might look at two or three different vehicles that have similar performance and cost. By examining why we find one car more appealing than the other, we start to distinguish its intangible value. It might be the brand that we think reflects the way we are, or that one company has a better record of sustainable manufacturing and recyclability. We notice the things we care about. Looking at alternatives in this way gives us an understanding of the intangible value that matters to us.

Next, what do our stakeholders value? In the last chapter, we distinguished between stakeholders in the decision and stakeholders of the decision. When we talk about stakeholder values, we're looking at stakeholders *of* the decision. This phase is an ideal opportunity to get to a common understanding of what value really looks like by bringing stakeholders of the decision together so that they can agree on the criteria.

Finally, trade-offs. When people hear the term trade-off, they tend to think about compromise – trying to have it all without giving anything up. I like to think of trade-offs as clean: if I'm going to do more of something, I've got to do less of something else. For example, a trade-off in terms of investment might be that you are going to invest more in one place and less in another without spreading your investment thinly across everything.

Similarly, there are trade-offs in aspects of value – what you might need to trade-off or 'give up' to deliver your outcome. This connects us with what we care about and helps us distinguish value. If we take our earlier example of the commercial real estate firm, there is a clear trade-off that stakeholders need to make between financial and environmental outcomes. To deliver the financial outcomes might require a certain level of investment and we will need to redirect that investment to deliver the environmental outcomes.

Foundations of the Prepare Value phase

These are the key foundations of this part of the Prepare phase:

1. **Treat value in its native form:** don't try to convert everything to a common financial metric. By treating value in this way, stakeholders will remain connected to the meaning of that value. If we talk about environmental sustainability, our relationship to that is quite different from a dollar representation of environmental sustainability, such as costs saved from kilogrammes of CO_2 not produced. Our relationship to dollars is

different from our relationship to environmental sustainability. We need to treat value in its native form.

2. **When articulating value, take a diverse range of perspectives:** particularly because we are trying to get to a commonly held view of value across our range of stakeholders and we cannot afford to miss a perspective.

3. **Break value into its component parts or dimensions:** this helps us be more specific about how we represent value and allows for the different perspectives to be represented explicitly.

4. **Be requisite in the number of criteria used:** it's tempting to capture too many criteria but this will result in paralysis by analysis. Good decision-making practice is to have only a handful of criteria for a significant decision. For example, in the NZDF case study, five criteria were used to represent the full spectrum of value that Defence delivers to stakeholders.

5. **Create a positive perspective:** think back to cognitive bias. Human beings are biased towards the status quo and have a loss aversion. We put more effort into holding onto something rather than moving forward. If we take a mixed positive and negative perspective, the decision is always going to be biased to the negative. This avoids losing something versus making a new investment. This does not mean ignoring the

negative consequences; instead, represent them in a positive sense – for example, a negative consequence might be reputational harm, and the positive view might be maintaining or enhancing reputation.

Prepare Value in practice

In this phase, we develop a set of criteria for our decision that represent the value that stakeholders care about and are requisite to help us make the decision. While tricky, this can be one of the most rewarding phases in the P^5 Framework because of the opportunity to engage stakeholders actively and have a strategic conversation about the environment in which we are making the decision. This is about helping structure our decision framework so that everyone is on board with it. Once stakeholders start to see the things that matter to them at a strategic level represented in criteria, they start to become committed to the decision process.

We typically start with a discovery step, where we look at what already exists in the organisation that might look like criteria – as with Plan, core documents such as the company strategy can help here. Remember: strategic objectives, KPIs, strategy pillars or the CEO's priorities are not criteria but they might be a good starting point. It is crucial that criteria are consistent with an organisation's purpose.

Following the discovery step, we hold stakeholder workshops so that we can understand their perspectives and get to a common view. Often the criteria development process starts with brainstorming as many different aspects of value as possible, asking stakeholders how the outcome of this decision will add value for them or their organisation. This facilitates the creation of several different characteristics of value.

The next stage is to group together similar ideas before turning this into a set of draft criteria. Each criterion is listed as a headline and then two or three paragraphs are written on each one that define what the criterion means. For example, ideas such as long-term value, future customer satisfaction and financial sustainability might be grouped together as a single 'future proofing' criterion. Having a clear, explicit and understandable description for each criterion is essential to help stakeholders have a common understanding of the criteria.

Each criterion gets worked up using a continuous review process and then these are signed off. As in the Plan phase, we identify who to involve and how. The sign-off (agreement) step is another great opportunity for stakeholder ownership and alignment.

Much like the Plan phase, Prepare Value needs to be given requisite time and energy, which for a major decision might require several workshops over some weeks. This time and effort investment is another key part of setting the decision process up for success.

JANE'S IT PROJECT PORTFOLIO CHALLENGE

Jane ran a short series of workshops with different mixes of stakeholders to develop criteria. Each workshop considered the questions: 'Why do we do IT projects?' and 'In what ways do IT projects provide value to stakeholders?' Over time the criteria were developed from simple one-word headlines into a clear, agreed set of headlines and descriptive text. Jane's criteria included aspects such as 'patient safety', 'health outcomes', 'patient experience' and 'business benefits'. The IT governance board agreed that the criteria were so important that they had the senior leadership team (which included the CEO) sign them off. This indicated there was clear commitment and support to the decision process from the most senior leaders in the health board.

Attributes of good criteria

It can be tempting to shortcut this phase and use your current strategic objectives as criteria, but it is important to remember that the decision-making process and the strategy development process are different. However, strategic objectives are a good source for developing criteria.

Good criteria need to be complete and represent all aspects of value that stakeholders care about. This is important because you don't want decisions over-turned later when a stakeholder says that something they cared about was not considered. We need to test our criteria to ensure that everything is included.

In general, criteria tend to fall into three main areas:

- Benefits

- Risks

- Costs

To be useful in the decision-making process, criteria need to be:

- **Strategic:** and come from all key stakeholders of the decision.

- **Requisite in number:** five to ten for a major portfolio decision.

- **Easily understood:** hence why we structure them as a headline followed by paragraphs. Any stakeholder reading the criteria will understand what's behind them, what's excluded and what makes them different from one another.

- **Mutually preference-independent:** there should be no double counting of preference between criteria. This is one reason why strategic objectives aren't criteria, because often there is an overlap of preference between them. If stakeholders can only determine their preference for an alternative against a criterion by reminding themselves of their preference for that same alternative against another criterion, the criteria are not preference-independent.

- **Non-redundant:** decision theory will tell us that any variable that is common across all our alternatives is not a valid basis for making a decision. If all our alternatives deliver the same value against one of our criteria, that criterion is not useful for decision making. It is helpful to develop our criteria in parallel with the Prepare Alternatives phase because we can start to test them with our alternatives. Sometimes we may include criteria that don't appear to be redundant at first but turn out to be redundant later in the decision process once we understand the range of alternatives we are considering.

Sometimes organisations take another organisation's criteria because they worked for them. Having read this chapter, you can see that criteria are specific to the decision, to the organisation, the stakeholders and the context of the decision. Taking someone else's criteria is highly unlikely to get to a result that is relevant for the specific decision being made. This is why I'm not supplying a template for criteria development; they need to be developed with a specific decision process in mind.

Having said that, criteria tend to fall into a number of natural types:

- Financial
- Internal, eg staff, culture or internal values
- External, eg customers, users or suppliers
- Long-term, eg future proofing or long-term success

As you can see, these areas give quite a good balance across the main concerns of an organisation.

Let's take a moment to look at the issue of risk in decision making. Many organisations will think of criteria as risks. In fact, it might look like their agenda is to minimise risk, not to maximise benefit. The more we focus on risk, the more we reinforce our loss aversion cognitive bias and the harder it becomes to make decisions that help provide change in moving forward. One could consider the corollary to risk as a benefit. If we assume that some risk has transpired, then the corollary benefit could be thought of as the value of recovering from that situation. Often in developing criteria we end up with a long list of risks we would want to review according to the positive view of having that risk not transpire. This is not to say we shouldn't consider risk explicitly in good decision making but to caution against over-focus on risk and to try to adopt that positive mindset where possible. In some cases, it may be appropriate to consider risks directly as criteria.

Examples of real criteria that have been used in decision-making processes:

- An organisation prioritised a number of competing research and development projects against a limited budget. The criteria headlines they used were revenue, profit, innovation, people, efficiency, and customer trust.

- A New Zealand district health board were prioritising capital investments. Their criteria headlines were population health improvement, treatment and recovery, patient safety, business benefits, and cost savings.

- When making major strategic decisions, defence organisations typically use criteria in the form of: safety and security, regional stability, global order, significant relationships, and future proofing.

Beneath each criterion there were two or three paragraphs of text that described the criterion in more detail, often including particulars of what was included and excluded so that the distinction between them was clear. The list of criteria and the descriptions should fit on a single A3 page. If they don't, your level of detail is too great or you have too many criteria.

CASE STUDY – HOW TO TURN THE BUSINESS AROUND?

Earlier, we described a large UK company, a subsidiary of a global corporation, and how they shifted their business from negative growth to putting millions onto their bottom line. When they worked through the Prepare Value phase, their main concerns were revenue and profit and their decision making was based entirely on these. They asked their stakeholders what they cared about. After discussion, it became clear that while they did care about revenue and profit, they also cared about innovation, customer satisfaction, reputation and long-term sustainability. By asking this question, they shifted from simply looking at financial outcomes to making important decisions against a set of tangible and intangible criteria. Once they were worked up and signed off, they became an invaluable lens for the organisation when considering what they should continue, what they should invest further in and what they should stop.

Avoiding pitfalls

The following are the key pitfalls to watch out for when developing criteria:

- **Too low-level criteria:** it is important to remember a requisite number here and keep them sufficiently strategic.

- **Using incomplete criteria:** criteria missing some aspect or value. They need testing before sign-off.

- **Double counting value:** outcomes will be skewed if they are double counted across multiple criteria.

- **Not giving criteria due consideration:** this is one of the most critical aspects of the framework and it is worth investing effort to make the criteria work well.

- **Anything will do:** remember, simply picking your strategic objectives or taking someone else's criteria doesn't work.

- **Assuming what stakeholders want without asking them:** they need to own the criteria.

- **Not wanting to get senior sign-off on your criteria:** or having leaders sign off the criteria without understanding how they will be used. This exposes your decisions to the risk later that individuals will not agree to the recommendations being made.

- **Weighting the criteria at this point in the process (it comes later in the Prioritise phase):** remember our principle of process before content. If you weight criteria too soon, you will start to get into the content of the decision of why one criterion might be more important than another. Or, more likely, weighting will be done incorrectly.

Reflection

1. Review your organisation's strategic objectives and consider the ways in which they represent the value to stakeholders, and the ways they don't.

2. Write down a list of stakeholders you might find helpful to engage with regarding defining value and developing criteria for your organisation.

Summary

The Prepare Value phase is about distinguishing, articulating and agreeing a common basis for evaluating our alternatives. This is a great opportunity for stakeholder engagement and participation and ensuring that what we're developing is requisite to making our decision and that there is a high level of sign-off at the end.

Don't forget that criteria are specific to a particular decision, organisation and context; do not skip over this phase and take someone else's criteria.

Well-articulated, agreed criteria that capture all aspects of value that our stakeholders care about will give us a solid, defensible framework to make our decision.

In Chapter 5 we will look at the second part of the Prepare phase. This is when we consider what our alternatives in the decision might be – what we often consider as the second of the two main 'inputs' to decision making.

5

Prepare Alternatives

What does a good alternative look like?

The second part of the Prepare phase covers the alternatives. Alternatives are the 'what' of a decision. What are the things that we are deciding between? We will also look at the trade-offs between the different things we could do. Much like Prepare Value, the process of identifying alternatives and articulating them is a great opportunity for creativity. It is crucial to go from being creative into a level of structure that then supports our next phase, Prioritise.

In dealing with alternatives, there are two areas we need to think about. The first is what those alternatives might look like. The second is the data we will need to help define our alternatives to make them useful in a decision process.

There are many different types of alternatives and they will depend critically on the decision that is being made. In the table below, you can see the alternatives that might be relevant in the different example decisions we looked at in Chapter 3.

Decision	Alternatives
What projects do we need to approve/reject?	The list of projects
Which strategic initiatives will deliver the vision?	A list of ideas from the strategy development process
Which activities are aligned with company and staff values?	The activities that the company is already delivering
Which products or markets should we exit and which should we focus on?	Our suite of products or a list of markets that we are in and new markets we could enter
Which investments will deliver the most and the least for public money?	The potential investments we could make

We talked about the concept of a decision model in Chapter 2. Alternatives are a key component of the decision model. Depending on the type of decision model, our alternatives might look different. In this book we are focusing on the model of portfolio prioritisation, picking many from many. We solve our decision problem through the sum of multiple alternatives.

Types of alternatives

Let's consider the alternatives that apply with different types of decisions:

- **Acquisition decision:** alternatives might be technical solutions or proposals from potential suppliers, or the suppliers themselves. A large New Zealand government department was buying a multimillion-dollar IT system. Their alternatives were responses to their call for proposals from major IT suppliers.

- **The business case:** alternatives might be different technical solutions to solving the problem. When the Royal New Zealand Air Force needed to upgrade their pilot training aircraft, the alternatives they considered were different types of aircraft and different ways of delivering pilot training.

- **The savings-type decision:** these alternatives could be activities we could stop or reduce. The NZDF example demonstrates this well, as the alternatives they were considering were levels of outcome in different areas of the organisation.

- **The project portfolio:** alternatives could be a list of IT projects or innovation projects. A commercial real estate firm wanted to review their innovation pipeline. Alternatives were generated through an ideation process and were the ideas they could potentially pursue.

- **A system of systems decision:** the alternatives might look like different levels or quality of system. When the Royal Navy needed to design a new frigate, the Type 26, the alternatives they decided upon were different types of weaponry, accommodation, engines, etc.

- **The strategic planning decision:** alternatives might be initiatives to help deliver on strategic objectives. Victim Support in New Zealand developed alternatives that included many different ways to deliver their five-year vision and shape their organisation.

You can choose to have sub-alternatives, too. These could be to continue or stop the project or reduce or increase the amount you invest in it. Alternatives aren't all or nothing. They can be a sliding scale. That helps us in our decision process, particularly to overcome our cognitive bias towards the status quo.

In decision modelling, alternatives are the trade-offs between what we could do, as opposed to the criteria representing the trade-offs between the value we get (*why* we do something). With portfolio-type decisions, there are often various areas of the decision and different outcomes in each area. For example, if our decision is a strategic planning decision, it will involve areas of our organisations such as sales, marketing, operations, production, each having different alternatives for that particular area. Thinking about decisions in this way helps to be clear about the complexity in our decision. In the New Zealand Defence Force example, there were twenty-three different areas of activity, each with around ten alternatives for every area, which equates to 230 alternatives across the whole of the NZDF. This allowed them to break their problem down into manageable chunks.

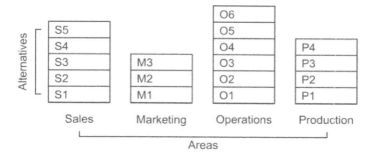

Figure 5.1: Example portfolio decision model showing eighteen alternatives grouped into four areas

But how many alternatives are needed? There is no hard-and-fast number. We need to consider the size of the problem we're dealing with. We want a sufficient number of alternatives so that we don't find ourselves forcing a decision outcome, but not so many as to get lost. Ideally you should be able to get the organisation onto one page. When we talked about New Zealand defence with twenty-three areas and ten levels, you could print that on a double A3 sheet of paper and there, in one view, is the entire organisation.

Ensure you have enough alternatives to solve your problem. For example, if your challenge is to save $10 million in operating costs and your alternatives are ideas for savings, those alternatives need to add up to much more than $10 million, otherwise you don't have sufficient alternatives to solve a $10 million problem. In general, we want at least twice as many alternatives as the size of the problem we are trying to solve.

Using a zero-based approach to making decisions gives an opportunity to look for options that might actually do *more* in certain areas than currently. The NZDF took a zero-based approach, which meant that some of their alternatives provided greater outcomes than their current Defence Force. Using this approach, they overcame people thinking that all they wanted to do was to cut or take money away from departments.

This negative mindset doesn't create a positive environment and can lead to behaviours where people put savings alternatives on the table but then argue that these can't be taken because of some 'must-do' or 'compliance' issue. A zero-based approach forces everyone to consider all possible savings and assume they have been taken, then take a positive approach of 'buying back' these alternatives and potentially also taking some alternatives beyond saving. The same approach can be used from a 'near zero' base, where we start from the irreducible minimum in each area, but not quite doing absolutely nothing.

Questions to ask in the Prepare Alternatives phase

1. What alternatives do we have?

2. What would they cost?

3. Who will be impacted by the alternatives?

4. What else is affected in my organisation?

5. How many alternatives do we need to ensure we can solve the challenge?

6. What other data do we need to support our alternatives?

7. Who could be involved in helping to design and set up our alternatives?

Foundations of the Prepare Alternatives phase

These are the key foundations that underpin this phase:

1. **Make alternatives 'hypothetically independent and mutually exclusive':** imagine you could pick any one of those alternatives but that choice doesn't require you to know which other ones you've picked. This will break through the complexity in our problem. Note the term 'hypothetically' here; inter-dependencies almost

always exist in the real world, but the key is to address them later (in the Package phase).

2. **Look widely for alternatives and be innovative:** this is to ensure you have plenty of alternatives to help solve your problem. Be broad in your search rather than finding just one or two answers.

3. **Frame your alternatives in a common way:** if you're dealing with a savings challenge, don't mix savings and investment terminology because our 'loss aversion' cognitive bias will mean we are biased against the savings versus the investment. Instead, frame savings as 'buy back' alternatives from the assumption you have already taken the saving.

4. **Iterate the alternatives:** exclude some that might be completely infeasible or generate new ideas from the current alternatives, perhaps by reviewing them against the criteria and seeing gaps in value. This is an iterative process that allows us to build a rich set of alternatives.

5. **Have an outcomes focus to alternatives:** define your alternatives from the outcomes they provide, not the details of what to do. Many organisations find this difficult.

6. **Define your alternatives with clear scale and scope:** in this way, the depth of the effect of the alternative, and its scope of impact, the breadth, is clear. This also allows for requisite cost information to be gathered.

If you ask people to come up with alternatives, for example about an IT project, they often simply say that this specific new platform 'must be implemented'. But that is not being outcome focused. It is a focus on 'how' we are going to do something. The outcome-focused approach might be to say: 'This new platform will support improved business efficiency.' We need an outcome focus so that we can compare alternatives with each other, which is what we will do in the Prioritise phase. The clearer we can get with defining our alternatives with an outcome focus, the easier it will be when we move into making decisions.

As organisations get used to these kinds of decision processes, they start to build experience and ability to articulate outcomes, and that pays dividends in many other areas of the organisation. When we define our alternatives, we want to articulate them in a preference-independent way – not a sales pitch such as: 'You must buy this IT system.' This sales pitch will directly trigger our cognitive biases around anchoring and maintaining the status quo. Articulate your alternatives in a balanced, factual, preference-independent way.

JANE'S IT PROJECT PORTFOLIO CHALLENGE

Jane already had a wide range of alternatives – around forty project requests from across the health board – but they were in varying levels of completeness and detail. Jane developed a standard one-page template and had the sponsor for each project complete it, including consistent project cost and resourcing projections. Jane's team supported the sponsors in creating factual, outcome-focused descriptions for each project so they were all defined in a comparable way. The team became practised at helping define IT projects using outcome-focused language: 'By upgrading to version 2.2, we will be able to operate in these different ways, with this many people benefitting.' This was a big improvement on typical ways of describing IT projects, for example: 'We must upgrade to version 2.2, it's the latest and best.' The IT governance board signed all the alternatives off before prioritisation.

How to develop alternatives

The choice of how to develop alternatives is dependent on the decision. For example, if your decision is about innovation projects that have come from a process to generate ideas then the alternatives may have already created themselves. Alternatives may also come out of your standard strategy process.

The two parts of this phase often happen in parallel because you may have conversations around strategic objectives and values to develop criteria, while having conversations about initiatives that would be our alternatives. Often criteria can give ideas of alternatives. For example, if we care about environmental efficiency, this might lead us to think of initiatives we could put in place to save energy or increase recycling. Understanding our criteria can give ideas for alternatives.

The following is a typical approach to developing alternatives:

1. Define the type of alternatives that will meet your objective – options for savings? New initiatives? Potential investments? This may also include groups or areas of alternatives (business units, functions, teams, etc).

2. Define what an alternative looks like – data needed, the size and scale of an alternative, the timing, etc.

3. Idea generation – a process whereby you call for proposals or ideas or run workshops to support alternative creation. This is a good place to use the criteria being developed in the Prepare Value phase to prompt new ideas for alternatives.

4. Shape those ideas into a consistent form – use a mini business case template that includes the name and owner of each alternative, a description of the outcome the alternative provides, how it will deliver that outcome, narrative on the risk of not taking the alternative, a list of people who might be affected, financial projections to execute this alternative and its financial returns and finally how the alternative will impact on our criteria.

5. Gather and prepare requisite data – develop the alternative by turning it from one line in a spreadsheet to the mini business case.

6. Sign-off – consider who's going to sign off and whether this is a governance responsibility. This is a critical last step in this phase and can ensure stakeholder ownership of the alternatives and support for the evolving decision process as a whole.

This is another great opportunity for active stakeholder participation, such as running workshops to generate ideas and develop them. Stakeholders can produce data that supports alternatives and may be involved in the sign-off of ideas, too. Alternatives may be captured or sourced from within enterprise-based IT tools such as project management or enterprise resource planning (ERP) systems. Because organisations often source data for alternatives from those systems, they may provide a clear, consistent place to collect and manage your alternatives.

What data do we need?

When working up alternatives, we need to think about the requisite level of data. The finance team or technical people in your organisation will want to provide you with reams of data, detailed analysis, thousands of lines of spreadsheets; in most cases that's over the top. As the decision process progresses, it becomes clearer what data is requisite and most often this can be gathered later (such as in the Package phase).

To support alternatives in a decision process, there are two distinct purposes for data:

1. **Reaching the decision:** we need data that supports making the decision, such as a whole-of-life cost estimate for the alternative, or data on the risk of not investing, or the scale and scope of the impact of the alternative. This includes narrative as well as numbers.

2. **Planning for execution:** this is data about the consequence of putting the alternative into practice, eg timing, resource requirements or year-on-year financial projections.

The key is to have comparable data across our alternatives so that we can compare them on a similar basis. Firstly, what's going to support the decision we're about to make? When we get to the Prioritise phase, you'll see how that data can support the decision. Secondly, we need to know what the future will look like if we take particular alternatives. This will be important in planning for execution, when we start to package up alternatives into future scenarios in the Package phase.

Data on the costs of alternatives can be broader brush to help us reach a rigorous decision that we will need once we start to develop an execution plan. Even rough cost estimates may be sufficient to help make a decision. When you start to plan execution, you can add more detail at that point. You might have many roughly costed alternatives, which will be sufficient to execute the Prioritise phase. During the Package phase, you will only need to work up detailed costing on some of those alternatives. An important consideration is not to bias the decision process towards alternatives that have more data available – the presence or absence of data does not necessarily make an alternative more or less attractive.

Gathering requisite data to support the decision is often challenging because typical financial systems don't support costing in a way that's useful for alternatives. If we're trying to define an alternative as an outcome, several activities may be needed to deliver that outcome, which all have a cost associated with them. Most financial accounting systems don't support activity-based costing, so work will be required on them to help identify and develop the costing relevant for alternatives. This is eminently solvable and many organisations have found a sensible way through it.

The principle of requisite data also applies to the financial return aspect. Highly detailed financial returns are not needed. There will be levels of uncertainty around those financial returns but requisite is the watch word for the level of data needed.

We need to consider risk here, too. One risk in a decision process is that you will not get the outcome you want or expect. Having rough data for costs and financial outcomes, tempered by an estimate of the probability of success, is one way of managing that risk. Always ensure you include your widest set of alternatives, even if you don't have detailed data to support them. You can apply a probability of success, which might be lower for less well-defined alternatives because you're uncertain about the data. Care is needed not to create a portfolio that has a risk imbalance.

CASE STUDY – WHICH MAJOR INVESTMENTS TO MAKE ACROSS GOVERNMENT?

A major government department wanted to improve the decision process for major investments and identified structured decision making, based on the P^5 Framework, as an appropriate tool to make cross-government decisions and trade-offs. A key part of this work was the identification of the alternatives. A call for information was issued across government asking what major investments were anticipated in a specific period to address expected gaps in government capability or upcoming risks.

Firstly, they created a clear definition of what an alternative looked like and then developed a template for alternatives, which included: the outcome of making this investment; what the investment comprised; the costs over time; what the risks were if they didn't make the investment; and the alternative 'owner'. They then provided the template to all the organisations concerned as a way of gathering consistent information about alternatives. Once the alternatives were received, they reviewed each of them and requested further information if it was needed by going back to the owner.

Avoiding pitfalls

1. **Under- or over-estimating costs:** both of these can mean the alternative will not be properly funded. Independent costing or cost assurance can help. The key is transparency.

2. **Costing that isn't independent between our alternatives:** alternatives should be hypothetically independent and mutually exclusive. We need to cost them in that way so we can meaningfully compare them – sometimes this may require making working assumptions, which can be revisited later during Package.

3. **Having a long list of 'must-do' alternatives:** this reduces our ability to solve our problem.

4. **Not including 'business as usual' in alternatives:** it's tempting to say that 'business as usual' activities don't count and that you are only looking for new initiatives but this usually does not solve the problem. Considering existing activities alongside new potential activities provides greater opportunity.

5. **Having too much data:** this will get us over-fixated on the numbers; be clear what is requisite

data at the start of this phase and only capture that.

6. **Alternatives described as a sales pitch:** focus on factual details and outcomes.

7. **'Artificial' alternatives:** these are put in to bias a decision-maker towards the result that we want. We've all seen this in business cases where there's the 'real' alternative we're recommending, the option that's so expensive it's unaffordable and the option that's so cheap it doesn't actually solve the problem. Those are not three alternatives. That is one alternative.

Reflection

1. Look at your standard business case template and review it in the light of this chapter. Does it focus on outcomes and does it require requisite data to support it?

2. When making a major decision, how many alternatives do you consider and are they real alternatives?

3. List the alternatives in a decision that you're facing or have faced and consider the criteria you will use for that decision. Look at the previous chapter and think of as many new alternatives again as you've already listed.

Summary

In this chapter we've covered what alternatives look like and the different types of alternatives that might be appropriate for different decisions. We've looked at the principles of those alternatives, in particular the need to be outcomes focused.

We've considered how to prepare alternatives and the data required to support the decision and understand the consequences.

Finally, we've considered some of the pitfalls in developing alternatives.

In short, a broad set of agreed, well-developed alternatives accompanied with requisite data and clear, non-salesy descriptive information will give us the best chance of solving our original challenge.

In Chapter 6 we will move on to the Prioritise phase, which is a key element of the P^5 Framework. This is the phase where we will prioritise and identify which alternatives will best achieve our outcomes.

6
Prioritise

Why prioritise?

Prioritisation is one of the most crucial factors of the P^5 Framework in ensuring better decision making. Having executed both parts of the Prepare phase, you should now be in a good position to prioritise. This is where the two core components of decision making, the criteria and the alternatives, come together – by considering how each of the alternatives will perform against each of the criteria.

Prioritisation is a key part of decision making because the decision emerges from the process of prioritisation. We should never ask simply whether we do something or not. Instead we should consider a range of alternatives. On completing this phase, it will be apparent which alternatives will best achieve the balance of outcomes we want. We don't just think of which are the least or most preferred alternatives. We want to know by how much one alternative stands out above the others and why. Many think of prioritisation as simply ranking options in a list, but the distance between one and two or three and four and so on is also helpful in decision making.

By the end of Prioritise we should have an agreed order of priority of our alternatives. Once we've got to that point, much of the difficult and contentious work in decision making is done.

Questions to ask in the Prioritise phase

Many of the core questions we might want to ask in executing the Prioritise phase have already been answered in Plan, but there are other questions that might help us implement Prioritise effectively:

1. How will I evaluate my alternatives against my criteria?

2. What kind of numbers or scoring system might I use to represent my evaluation?

3. What kind of tools might support my prioritisation?

4. How will I have my stakeholders agree on the prioritisation?

Foundations of the Prioritise phase

The four core principles of Decision Thinking underpin the Prioritise phase as this is such a pivotal piece in the decision-making jigsaw and they are joined by some additional foundations. The following foundations underpin the Prioritise phase:

1. **Academically rigorous process:** using a structured, clear, repeatable and accurate process backed by academic research can make the difference between a meaningful outcome and something that no one agrees with or just becomes undone later once challenged.

2. **Start with expansive thinking:** apply the constraints at the end of our prioritisation process – do not limit our set of alternatives before we start.

3. **Break the problem into manageable pieces:** in Chapter 2 we introduced the concept of decision modelling to break things down; this includes breaking prioritisation into manageable steps and sets of conversations.

4. **Continued stakeholder participation:** we can have this participation at different parts of our prioritisation activity.

5. **Never ask what's 'more important':** the answer will emerge through a good prioritisation process. We don't want to get anchored (a common

cognitive bias) before we start by pre-empting the answer.

6. **Prioritisation isn't the answer:** it's a helpful step towards the answer and hence it's not the last of our phases.

7. **Prioritise alternatives based on value per unit of 'constraint':** for example, if the constraint is an investment budget, prioritise on value for money – this is where we capitalise on the work preparing our alternatives.

Prioritisation in practice

There are two sides of the prioritisation coin. Firstly, there is the theory, which I call the 'technical' process of prioritisation. Secondly, there is the practice, which is the 'social' process of prioritisation. The technical process helps us get to the answer, while the social process helps us get to the commitment, and together they lead to better decision making. I strongly recommend this socio-technical approach for prioritisation; it's the key to decisions that stick. There are many elegant, purely technical decision support processes out there, but without the social aspects of decision making the real outcomes of the decision often aren't achieved.

Let's look at a real-life example – the digital transformation initiatives that many companies are implementing. Business leaders often struggle to choose which business problems to solve, and which problems are a good fit for the data, artificial intelligence (AI) and machine learning (ML) models. Traditionally, a simple two by two matrix is used (feasibility and impact) to evaluate AI use cases, but this is insufficient and often results in failure of these technical projects.

Investa, a forward-thinking commercial property company, has used rigorous prioritisation within a P^5 Framework-based process to build an AI/ML use case evaluation tool. They have created world-leading solutions, which have resulted in new opportunities and growth.

Evaluating alternatives – the technical process

There are many ways to evaluate the alternatives from the Prepare Alternatives phase against our outcomes (our criteria). We could rely on our old friend, the coin toss, but much more effective is a methodology called multi-criteria decision analysis (MCDA), created by leading academic institutions in the US and the UK more than forty years ago. MCDA helps compare a range of often dissimilar alternatives using the common metric of value added. This idea of value added is as we defined it in the Prepare Value phase discussed in Chapter 4.

There are two core activities in an MCDA process. The first is 'scoring' an alternative against each of the particular criteria. This means determining a numerical value (the score) that represents how much value that alternative provides against that criterion. To be precise, the score is a 'preference value' because it represents your preference for the value the alternative provides against that criterion.

The second core activity is 'weighting', which is scaling the criteria scores for each option to combine them into a single value, creating a single overall representation of the value added by the alternative while allowing for the different value contributions of the criteria.

This weighted scoring system is common. You may have used this technique in your own decisions. Sometimes with poorly designed or executed weighted scoring systems, all the alternatives end up looking equally attractive or several alternatives seem to have the same priority and, in these cases, decision making becomes harder, not easier.

Scoring

For MCDA to effectively support better decision making it needs to be technically sound and there are many important and often subtle considerations, most of which are beyond the scope of this book. Here are a few that are commonly missing:

- The scoring scale (often 'high, medium, low' or 'zero to five') needs to allow for sufficient discrimination between the actual value each of the alternatives provides. For example, an option may deliver three times the value against one criterion compared to another; a three-point scale of zero, one or two wouldn't allow for that difference to be represented.

- The increase in preference value from one scoring point to the next needs to be the same across all points. For example, the difference in preference value between a score of one and two (a one-point difference) needs to be the same as the increase in value between a score of four and five. This is called an interval scale.

- The score is a representation of value, not the value itself. Celsius is a representation of temperature – it isn't the temperature. When we talk about value, we mean how much we care about something, our 'preference'. Often alternatives may have data, but the data is not necessarily the same as the score. We might care that a building we invest in has a greater than four-star energy efficiency rating, but as long as it's at least four stars, we might not really care whether it's 4, 4.5 or 5. However, we might care a lot that it's at least a three-star energy rating and therefore our preference value (score) for any rating lower than three stars would be much lower than our score for four. In this case the data (the star rating) is not the preference value.

Figure 6.1: Our preference for building energy efficiency rating may not be the same as the star rating

This all shows us that when designing the prioritisation technical process, we need to consider the criteria scales we will use to score our alternatives against.

One of the most helpful ways of scoring alternatives is to use an approach called relative preference scoring. Here, we compare our alternatives against each other and then ascribe scores that relate to our preference for the relative value each option provides against that criterion. Our brains are good at making comparative (relative) judgements but not good at making absolute judgements. Using this relative approach is helpful in having our brains do their best work.

Weighting

Similar principles apply when we are weighting criteria and we decide on the different relative value our criteria provide for our overall decision. Most weighted scoring systems don't use this level of rigorous consideration of relative preference. When I started working in this field, I set myself the (secret) mission to fix the world's bad scoring systems, because most break the core principles.

Once we've defined rigorous scales and a good process to do the scoring and we recognise that scores in themselves aren't data, that they can represent anything, tangible or intangible, we're in good shape. Now we have a common basis for comparing our intangible and tangible value, which is one of our core principles. As long as we have clear alternatives and well-founded criteria, hence the Prepare phase, MCDA can break our problem down into pieces, one criterion at a time.

Howard Raiffa, one of the earliest and leading academics in the world of decision science, noted in his 1968 book *Decision Analysis*:

'The spirit of decision analysis is divide and conquer: decompose a complex problem into

simpler problems, get one's thinking straight
on these simpler problems, paste these anal-
yses together with logical glue, and come
out with a program of action for the complex
problem.'

With this approach, we never have to say which alternative is better overall. We only ever compare alternatives one criterion at a time. Once we've determined
the scores and have the weights, and we multiply our
scores by the weights, the prioritisation emerges. The
programme of action starts to become apparent.

This approach to scoring keeps us in a positive mindset
and makes it easier for people to engage in the process
because they will think about the value something
provides against the criteria and not whether we
should or shouldn't do something.

With a clear set of consistent scores against each criterion, and weights for our criteria, we can then add
up the weighted scores and, hey presto, we'll have
a 'weighted preference score' for each of our alternatives, and hence an order of priority. This order
of priority shows the options with the most and the
least value across all our criteria. That's a huge step
forward from a random list.

Order of priority and sensitivity analysis

If we want to prioritise on the basis of value for money, we now have a single number per alternative that represents our preference for the total value provided, which we can divide by the cost of executing that alternative. We can then list the alternatives in order of value divided by money, where the number one rated alternative provides the best value for money. Those that provide the least value for money will come at the bottom of the list; these are often the items that deliver the least value and also happen to be the most expensive. Now we have prioritised, we can select the best alternative or set (portfolio) of alternatives from the top down.

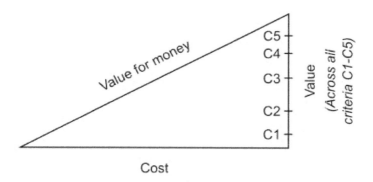

Figure 6.2: The value for money of an alternative is the slope of the triangle, the steeper the better

Now we have an order of priority: a clear distinction between all our alternatives and a clear view of why one is preferred over another. The different criteria scores might show that one alternative is strong in one area and weak in another area. Because of this technically sound process, we can perform a sensitivity analysis. Here we explore alternative scores or weights to see how robust the outcome is and what might cause the result to change.

It may be tempting to change the scores and weights on a table of MCDA data to see what makes a difference, perhaps to 'game' the result. But we need to ensure that when we do sensitivity analysis, we maintain a clear relationship between the numbers and the value against the criteria they represent. We will discuss sensitivity analysis further in the next chapter.

Dealing with uncertainty

When discussing value, we looked at how we might treat risks as criteria, and in this case we are dealing with risks as impacts, or effects of our actions. We also often consider uncertainty – the risk of not getting the outcomes we expect, for example. A helpful way to take uncertainty into account in our prioritisation is the approach of 'risk adjustment'. This is where we apply an uncertainty factor, often termed 'probability of success', to our weighted preference values for our alternatives. This gives us a 'risk-adjusted weighted preference value' and has the effect of reducing the value for money of more uncertain, or risky, alternatives. Figure 6.3 illustrates the effect of risk adjustment.

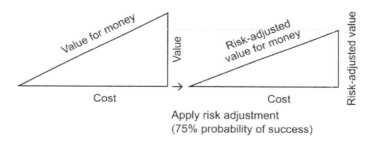

Apply risk adjustment
(75% probability of success)

Figure 6.3: Lower probability of success gives us lower risk-adjusted value for money, a shallower sloped triangle

It is common to use a software tool to support MCDA prioritisation, which ensures consistent use of the numbers and, critically, will provide a visualisation of the outcomes. Figure 6.4 shows a typical MCDA output that we refer to as a 'tornado'. We can see our alternatives listed in the order of priority from the top down. The different shaded bars show how well each alternative performs against our five criteria. You can see the relative value of the different alternatives on the right and their respective costs on the left. You can also see the effect of risk adjustment – the dashed areas on the value bars represent the level of risk adjustment.

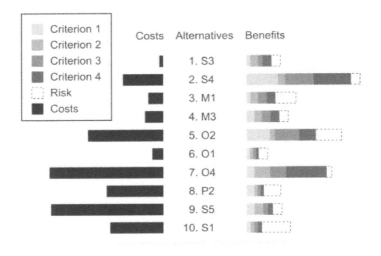

Figure 6.4: Example 'tornado' chart of value for money prioritisation

Decision Conferencing – the social process

The technical process, if using MCDA, is generally straightforward, as long as it's properly designed and executed. But what of the social process we referred to earlier? How do we get stakeholders to own the outcome so there is commitment to the decision and it sticks? If we look back to the core principle of active stakeholder participation, I recommend that stakeholders do the scoring and criteria weighting.

I've found Decision Conferencing, which was developed by Lawrence Phillips in the late 1970s, to be the most consistent and effective process, especially with groups of diverse stakeholders and complex decisions. A Decision Conference is a structured workshop to perform the actions of an MCDA prioritisation. The overall intent of a Decision Conference is to develop a shared understanding of the issues, a sense of common purpose and a commitment to action among stakeholders.

The Decision Conferencing approach includes the following fundamentals:

- Brings diverse stakeholders together.

- Involves a series of group discussions to score the options and weight the criteria using a carefully designed process. This helps stakeholders learn from each other's perspectives and come to a shared view of scores and weights.

- Uses independent facilitation, which is critical so that all voices can be heard, the facilitator can help manage the impact of bias and the processes are followed correctly.

Decision Conferencing in practice

A Decision Conference starts with an introductory briefing on the process and the overall 'context' to get clear on the environment being operated within and what you want to achieve. The 'rules of the game' and the roles in the room are also made clear at this point; this is crucial to distinguish the role of the facilitator as expert in the process and not in the content.

The roles required for the Decision Conference are:

- **Chair:** the chair is mostly an evaluator but occasionally helps break any impasse in the evaluators' discussion. The chair does not need to perform the 'usual' chair functions of a meeting – the facilitator takes care of those.

- **Evaluators:** they perform the scoring, weighting and other active parts of the process. All are considered 'equal'.

- **Subject matter experts (SMEs):** they brief the evaluators on the alternatives being evaluated and only answer questions/clarifications when called upon by the evaluators. They do not participate in scoring, weighting, etc.

- **Facilitator:** the facilitator is an expert in the Decision Conferencing process and must be independent from the chair, evaluators and SMEs. They manage the timeline, ensure all evaluators participate and get the conference to a positive conclusion. They do not participate in scoring or weighting or offer any opinions.

- **Analysts:** they support the facilitator and sometimes co-facilitate, and ensure all judgements (scores, weights, etc) are captured accurately.

They keep notes on pertinent rationale from the scoring and weighting and manage any software tools being used.

Other roles, such as scribes, facility administrators, etc, may be required depending on the size and nature of the conference.

Next the criteria are briefed to ensure a clear shared view of what each criterion represents and includes and excludes.

Following this the options are briefed. This is often done by SMEs on particular alternatives or proposals.

The conference then moves to facilitated discussions to agree the scores, which might be broken down by groups or areas of alternatives. Following scoring, weighting is agreed for the criteria.

The results are then reviewed live in the room. This is an important part of the Decision Conference as it ensures that everyone can see the results of the work they and others have done.

Finally, the participants agree the order of priority in principle.

There are many ways to structure Decision Conferences, including:

- Holding a one-day workshop with one set of stakeholders to work through all the steps

- Holding several workshops or Decision Conferences with sets of alternatives and then bringing the results together in a 'merge' conference

- Holding one Decision Conference that performs the scoring only, and another one with a more senior group of stakeholders to agree the weights

There are some key features of a Decision Conference that make it work, which you will recognise from the earlier discussions in this chapter:

- Never have a discussion about one alternative being better than another overall. Discussions are always broken down by criterion, which allows stakeholders to participate collaboratively, rather than fighting for their alternative over their neighbour's alternative.

- The agreed scores and weights are captured live into a tool, which means the results can be seen at the end of the day to ensure group ownership and to create an audit trail. This collaborative approach shifts the dynamic from people disagreeing with each other to the group collaborating on a common goal, as depicted by the model.

- Continued ownership by stakeholders throughout the process. If there are multiple workshops, there is common participation of one or two individuals and this results in ongoing ownership.

- Clearly defined roles in the room specifying what each person can and can't do, and how they can participate. As an example, the facilitator would never suggest scores or weights to the group.

- A Decision Conference is not like any other workshop or meeting. It's highly effective at having diverse groups collaborate and reach a shared decision. Everyone can see how their input is being considered and how the group reaches a conclusion.

- Sensitivity analysis is one of the most powerful techniques in a Decision Conference. If the group can't agree on a score, it's possible to capture one or two alternative scores that can then be tested through the MCDA sensitivity analysis process. This prevents one person becoming disenfranchised and disengaging from the process. For example, in one large government organisation, two senior stakeholders who owned their individual piece of the organisation would normally never be seen to agree with one another. But in a Decision Conference where they could see the scoring and the weighting process, one of them agreed to give up resources to the other.

Prioritisation is always a conversation about value against criteria and the shared result. The agreed result emerges over the course of the activity and everyone owns it.

JANE'S IT PROJECT PORTFOLIO CHALLENGE

The heart of Jane's decision process design was a Decision Conference involving members of the IT governance board and other relevant stakeholders such as the master planner. The chair of the IT governance board chaired the Decision Conference. It was important for Jane that there was a good balance of clinical and non-clinical participants. SMEs from the different clinical and business areas (such as surgery, general medicine, mental health, facilities management, HR) briefed each of the proposed projects and then the Decision Conference participants scored the proposals against the criteria and weighted the criteria. During scoring, the participants also agreed a percentage 'probability of success'. An MCDA decision model was used to capture the scores, probabilities of success and weights and to visualise the risk-adjusted order of priority at the end of the day. The Decision Conference was facilitated by an expert in MCDA and Decision Conferencing (me, as it happened). Throughout the day, any disagreements on scores and weights were either resolved through discussion or captured as alternatives for sensitivity analysis.

The Decision Conference reached a clear agreed order of priority of all the project proposals and all the stakeholders were positive about their experience, noting the value of the in-depth discussions during scoring and how it gave them a much clearer view of each proposal and a truly cross-health board perspective.

CASE STUDY – WHICH INNOVATION PROJECTS TO PURSUE?

Innovation 'ideas' are traditionally the pet projects of senior stakeholders, and decisions on which projects to prioritise and pursue are made in an ad hoc manner, largely behind closed doors. As a result, many innovative projects do not have the sponsorship, team or resources that they need to fully succeed. Corporate innovation often fails and that failure starts with the way that the innovation investment decisions were made. Investa built an innovation and decision intelligence function and created a robust innovation investment tool within a P^5 Framework process. This allowed the team and stakeholders to prioritise and agree on which ideas to pursue.

Joanna Marsh, General Manager of Innovation and Advanced Analytics at Investa, said:

'Corporate innovation very quickly becomes a problem of too many ideas, each vying for a limited pool of funding and resourcing. It is vital to make innovation investment decisions that align to the business strategy, and actually move the dial on business performance. Using structured decision making has allowed us to evaluate very different ideas across a standard set of criteria, and then focus to create some truly market-disrupting innovation.'

Avoiding pitfalls

Prioritisation can be a complex process. There are many ways it could go wrong, including the following:

1. **A lack of rigour or consistency in executing the process:** for example, if we don't define our scoring scales correctly, one set of scores against a criterion might not be relevant compared to another set.

2. **Having the wrong participants:** some people might not want to include a particular stakeholder because of concern that the stakeholder would upset the process, or junior substitutes are sent rather than senior representatives.

3. **Turning a Decision Conference into a pitching type activity:** this should be a balanced consideration of all the alternatives against the criteria. Alternatives should be presented in a factual way. It is not a chance to persuade the participants to support one alternative.

4. **Self-facilitation:** deciding not to have a facilitator never works because then everyone is a participant and the process can easily get off track.

5. **Using SMEs to facilitate or selecting a facilitator who cannot be impartial:** if the participants don't see the facilitator as impartial, the result may be invalidated due to perceived bias and the activity

may get stuck. The facilitator must come from outside the organisation or from part of the same organisation that is distant from the accountable decision-maker and participants.

6. **Not having a chair for workshops:** this role is distinct from the facilitator and ensures the facilitator can remain separate from the content but fully supported and empowered by the accountable decision-maker to make progress.

7. **Treating it as a numbers game with the sole aim of 'filling in the spreadsheet':** it is critical to understand the numbers associated with the MCDA process. They need to be treated with due consideration and care and not turned into a random number generator.

8. **Allowing insufficient time for the social process:** a crucial part of the social process is the shared understanding that emerges from appropriate levels of challenge and discourse. It's essential to avoid the temptation to 'fast track' the social process to save time.

Reflection

Have you used a scoring and weighting type approach to support prioritisation? If so, review it, asking yourself the following questions:

1. Did the scoring scales have enough points to reflect the scale and scope of value and differentiate the alternatives?

2. Was there a clear record or audit trail of how the scores and criteria weights were agreed?

3. Were appropriate stakeholders engaged in the processes of scoring and weighting?

4. When you looked at the results, how did you and stakeholders feel about them? Did they feel intuitive? Was it the kind of answer you were expecting? Could you see where surprises such as 'pet projects' scoring poorly came from? Now you understand more about scoring and weighting, see if you can see why the results were not intuitive.

Summary

In this chapter we have covered why prioritisation is necessary in decision making and the key foundations to make it successful. We have introduced the concept of a socio-technical process, in which the technical aspects help us get towards the answer and the social dimension gets the ownership and commitment.

We have also covered how MCDA can be a helpful technical methodology for rigorous prioritisation and how Decision Conferencing helps run an effective MCDA process.

Finally, we listed the pitfalls to watch out for. If I was to highlight one, it would be: don't treat prioritisation as a numbers game.

Using a technically rigorous methodology for prioritisation, with strong social process and stakeholder participation, will get us to an agreed and stakeholder-supported prioritisation of our alternatives.

In the next chapter, we will go into detail on the Package phase, where we start to develop our recommendations for the decision-makers.

7
Package

Why package?

You might think that the hard work of decision making is during the Prioritise phase and that we have now made the decision. We haven't. We've agreed the order of priority as an output of the Prioritise phase but now we will start to make the recommendations to the ultimately accountable decision-makers for the actual decision.

This Package phase varies depending on the kind of decision you are making. We are focusing our attention on 'portfolio prioritisation' decisions. In this type of decision, we look for the combination of options across our portfolio that gives us the best outcome – the 'proposed package'.

An organisation I worked with once said that the Package phase is where 'science meets art' in decision making. That's because during all of the other phases we have applied a technically rigorous, academically sound process through prioritisation. This has given us a robust hypothetical outcome, which we can now turn into something practical.

The Package phase should increase our confidence in our results and the decision that we're going to make. In the previous chapter, we talked about the sensitivity analysis that we can do as a way of helping stakeholders own the results and test alternative considerations that might come up during our prioritisation activity. This gives confidence in the results of prioritisation. Now we want confidence that the package we're putting forward is the strongest and the best outcome we can achieve.

It is also an opportunity to bring different people into the decision process, particularly as the results by definition are going to impact on the wider organisation. For example, we may need SMEs who have not been involved to date to bring their perspectives and expertise to the table, or we may want to 'red team' the work to test how well it stands up to challenge. This will ensure that the results of our decision making become integrated into the organisation because our commitment is the execution of the decision (the 'sticking' part), not just a hypothetical decision in and of itself.

The core inputs to the Package phase

1. **Input order of priority:** this is our initial order of priority. The Prioritise phase is structured so that the order of priority has a strong sense of ownership and commitment. This requires care because stakeholders can easily walk away from results if they do not feel ownership of them. As with all other phases, active stakeholder participation is another key part of the Package phase.

2. **Constraints:** in the Prepare phase, we talked about criteria and the things we valued and how these might look like constraints rather than criteria. There could be different alternative futures or scenarios that we need to explore, each with different constraints, such as financial budgets, timing, resource availability, etc.

3. **Data:** this is gathered during the Prepare Alternatives phase and includes data on financial implications, human resource requirements, implications of options, dependencies or impacts elsewhere in the business. Using this data effectively requires us to engage with SMEs for additional support as necessary.

4. **Other contexts:** other outputs from the Plan phase come back into play; for example, delivering what's needed for our business plan, the wider strategy, political consideration, etc. We also need to consider boundaries, particularly in the public

sector, such as policy considerations and whether it breaks any strategic requirements as we move from what looks good in principle towards something that works in practice.

Constraints versus criteria in decision making

There is a clear difference between what we call criteria, how we articulate value, and constraints. There is a sliding scale to criteria, which we can use to evaluate alternatives compared to each other. In Prepare, we considered constraints because we wanted to know whether some of our alternatives were completely unviable, and filter them out at that point. Although, we don't want to filter too heavily as one of our foundations is to have more alternatives to consider rather than fewer, which will give us better decision outcomes.

In Package, we return to those constraints. An obvious constraint might be a financial one, where we have a certain budget that we can't exceed. We need to apply the constraint of how much money we can spend. I frequently challenge organisations about how much the budget is a constraint. In the case study in Chapter 2, we met a clear constraint of a government department's level of funding but, after completing the process based on the P^5 Decision Framework, the government agreed to give them more money. Budget can look like a hard constraint to start with but once you've seen the results of structured decision making, the value of spending more can become clearer. Resourcing may be another constraint. Some projects may require a certain level of staffing to deliver them and be limited by organisation capacity.

Another example of this was when the Royal Navy were considering the design of the (at the time) new Type 45 destroyer. The problem started with the operational requirements as a stimulus for alternatives but turned into stakeholders treating operational requirements as hard constraints to protect their areas of the ship. This is a great example of how a structured decision process helped all stakeholders agree on the difficult trade-offs to design the best possible 'portfolio' of capabilities in a ship. The Type 45 case study was published in Chapter 3 of *Portfolio Decision Analysis: Improved methods for resource allocation* (edited by Salo, Keisler and Morton) and provides a detailed insight into this process in action.

While constraints don't help us differentiate between our alternatives, they do help us create a viable decision and way forward. Constraints can be more sophisticated than simply a number. A financial constraint might be a set of budget numbers over a period of time. The next five years might have different budget figures. The constraint isn't a single number. It's a financial profile. The same might go for people. Or the constraints might depend on the nature of the alternatives we are considering. For example, level of appetite for risk could be a constraint, but we might not know whether we meet or exceed that constraint until we've seen what alternatives we're considering.

When constraints are profiles over time, this is where the art side of the Package phase appears. You are no longer looking for the alternatives that add up to a particular total, you are looking for the best alternatives that give you this total with a particular profile over time. It then becomes a multi-dimensional problem that requires some art to solve.

Understanding value for money

In the Prioritise phase, we said that the most effective way to prioritise was to optimise on the value we get for a given constraint, which is most commonly value for money. Interpretations of what value for money looks like are wide-ranging. Many see it as fixed and that something is or is not value for money. In the world of structured decision making, value for money is a continuum and is often a basis for comparing alternatives. Our scores and our weighted criteria give us a common basis of value and we understand the investment required. Then we can calculate value for money. Figure 6.2 shows that value for money is the total value the alternative provides across all of our criteria divided by the cost of delivering that alternative. It's important to think about a total amount of value that an alternative will provide against our criteria over a period of time, for example three to five years.

We need to apply the same rigorous view to the money half of the equation, ensuring that if we talk about a three-year value we consider a three-year cost. We mentioned in Prepare Alternatives the requisite data required to support our alternatives and the whole-of-life cost or cost over a period of time. How do we consider value and money on the same basis, at the same time and with the same scope? Once we've done that, we can take the value and divide it by the money. This will give us the value for money ratio, which we can then prioritise on that basis. This is important so that we can start from the right place in our Package phase.

Questions to ask during the Package phase

1. Do I want several proposed packages or just one? This depends on the overall outcome from the decision. It might be a single recommendation or two or three different scenarios.

2. What are the constraints I'm dealing with? Are they hard constraints or just guidance?

3. Am I clear on the decision outcome from the Plan phase? This may have evolved over time and

require reviewing because we are about to build packages that deliver on that outcome.

4. Who are the right people to involve now? Make sure you have the right stakeholders involved, which may mean more business analysts or others from the organisation who have not participated in the decision process so far.

5. How do we demonstrate the consequences of our decision? This will come up in our next phase but you need to consider now what that presentation will look like and whether you are producing data that is appropriate.

Foundations of the Package phase

1. **Value for money guidance:** this is the value per unit of constraint, which might be value for money or value for people (head count). It's important to build your package guided by the item, eg value for money, and not on value alone.

2. **Make trade-offs:** don't just do everything. A common pitfall I see is that no one wants to say they are going to stop or not execute any of their alternatives so they end up doing everything badly.

3. **Prioritisation isn't the answer:** it's an input to and guidance for packaging. The Package phase

needs to start with prioritisation and then get to a practical solution.

4. **There is no single silver bullet solution:** this is an iterative process. Be prepared to evolve and continually involve stakeholders as you iterate.

Making trade-offs

According to Dictionary.com, a 'trade-off' is the exchange of one thing for another of more or less value to affect a compromise. I avoid the word compromise when thinking about trade-off because that often means no one is happy. To me, trade-off means getting to the best outcome by making specific choices. It is the exchange of one thing for another and not about cutting everything back a bit. It is far too common that organisations want to avoid difficult decisions by doing everything badly rather than the 'right' things well. This 'salami slicing' approach is seldom successful.

In Package, trade-offs are about selecting some alternatives over others. However, during this phase new alternatives can emerge. For example, we might discover that only one part of an alternative in our portfolio is driving the value of the alternative. We might choose to include a reduced scope alternative. That's fine so long as we can infer the value it provides from the work we did during Prioritise. Sometimes, instead of taking A or B, there is a case for taking a bit of A but you have to treat trade-offs as true exchanges rather than simply reducing things.

This approach to portfolio decision making also accommodates what economists call the 'opportunity cost' trade-off. As long as we have considered a wide enough range of alternatives, we can clearly see the opportunity cost of taking one alternative by the remaining alternatives we are now no longer able to take.

Packaging in summary

As one of the foundations of the packaging process is that it is iterative, we need to set aside a requisite amount of time for doing this. It is a common pitfall not to do this and instead build our overall decision process with the Prioritise phase late in the process, which reduces the amount of time we spend on the Package phase. Don't languish in this phase either because rapid iterations will help us make progress.

There are several key steps to take when putting this phase into action. Firstly, agree the basis for the proposed package with the key sponsor in a series of conversations or a workshop to get clarity on the constraints. It's critical that the key sponsor owns this because, if the results of the Package phase aren't presented in a way that is meaningful to them, we have wasted our time. We also need to know who to involve. Noting the level of iteration and analysis that may be needed, this will require those key participants to set aside time for this.

Secondly, we need to set up the business rules for the process. It is tempting to throw away all the good work from the earlier phases and turn it into a 'game of Tetris' and just pick the best answer you can, particularly if there are some stakeholders who weren't comfortable with the results. They may start making 'captain's picks' of the best answer. It's important to agree the business rules and be clear on the roles the stakeholders play before you start the packaging process.

The business rules and the plan we follow will start with the order of priority. We then apply our first constraint. We look at that as a 'candidate' package, applying other constraints, to see what difference that makes. We then revisit and iterate because this is now a multi-dimensional problem and a single constraint such as budget won't necessarily give us a meaningful outcome. Business rules should include the way we will operate and interact with the inputs. Our plan will include who will do what and when and, importantly, as we iterate the plan, who reviews and provides guidance about the results of the package drafts because questions will need to be answered and assumptions made about how we're proceeding.

We want agreement between each of the phases of the P⁵ Framework, and in the Package phase there are micro agreements because there can be a lot of data analysis and we want to ensure we are not on the wrong track.

Thirdly, we execute. How this looks is dependent on particular alternatives, the context and the decision itself.

Packaging in practice

A group of experts in the prioritisation work come together to ensure that all the work done previously is considered in a requisite way. Other experts in specific alternatives or strategy might also be involved who understand the wider scope and context of the business or the organisation. Analysts may analyse the packages to see what they look like in practice, such as considering the resource mix, the cost, the impact on other activities in the business and the change requirements to deliver those. We describe this process as generating our first candidate package option.

Steps to generate a candidate package option

1. **Build up until we've hit our constraint(s):** let's consider an investment situation with a budget constraint and let's use the example model in Figure 5.1. Starting at the top of our

value for money order of priority, we take each alternative in turn until all of our budget has been committed, let's say halfway down. This is our first candidate package option, shown in Figure 7.1. Analysts will compare the package to other constraints such as resources, or they might add up the change impact requirements to check that no other constraints have been broken. We might need to iterate here and remove some alternatives as, although we can afford to do the top half of our order of priority in terms of budget, we might not have the people (see Figure 7.2).

Order	Alternative	In?	
1	S3	✓	
2	S4	✓	
3	M1	✓	
4	M3	✓	
5	O2	✓	
6	O1	✓	
7	O4	✓	
8	P2	✓	
9	S5	✗	Budget constraint
10	S1	✗	
11	M2	✗	
12	P4	✗	
13	P3	✗	
14	O3	✗	
15	O6	✗	
16	S2	✗	
17	O5	✗	
18	P1	✗	

Figure 7.1: Order of priority of our eighteen alternatives with first candidate package option selected

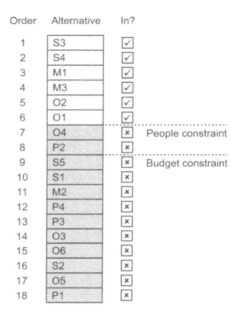

Figure 7.2: Modified candidate package option to meet people constraint

2. **Review dependencies:** we then look at dependencies, asking if it is possible to execute this candidate package option, remembering that when designing our alternatives and building our decision models all our alternatives have been created as hypothetically independent. It may be that you can't execute an alternative from the top half of your order of priority without an alternative from lower down (a dependency), below the line we've drawn. It's critical that we don't 'blow the budget' by just adding that alternative in. We will need to go above our line and decide which ones

we are going to remove. Imagine the line is now drawn at the sixth alternative but we might add an alternative after that for dependency reasons. We will then need to go back to item 6 and work up from there, removing alternatives from the package as appropriate (see Figure 7.3). This is what we mean by trade-off. Maybe we've traded in item 12 and traded out items 4 and 5. For example, above the line, you might decide to buy new helicopters. The helicopters are only useful if a ship takes them to where they need to be used. But all your ships might be in the bottom half of the priority order.

Order	Alternative	In?	
1	S3	✓	
2	S4	✓	
3	M1	✓	
4	M3	✗	traded 'out'
5	O2	✗	traded 'out'
6	O1	✓	
7	O4	✗	People constraint
8	P2	✗	
9	S5	✗	Budget constraint
10	S1	✗	
11	M2	✗	
12	P4	✓	traded 'in'
13	P3	✗	
14	O3	✗	
15	O6	✗	
16	S2	✗	
17	O5	✗	
18	P1	✗	

Figure 7.3: Modified candidate package option with trade-offs due to dependency on alternative 12

3. **Consider other constraints:** we need to consider all these constraints and ensure we have helpful business rules in place. You can always iterate between the Package and Prioritise phases. We can look at a candidate package option in Package and then revisit Prioritise to see if anything has changed as a result of dependency considerations, or perhaps cost efficiencies as a result of selecting a number of related alternatives.

4. **Compare to the hypothetically 'best' package:** we may now compare the candidate package option to the hypothetically best value for money option. That might inform us whether we've moved so far away from the best solution that it's now becoming unattractive to us.

5. **Test the Package option with stakeholders:** as well as our governance arrangements to ensure their continued ownership of the work we're doing. This is where the science starts to move into the art. Now it looks like a technically sound prioritisation that has had judgement and a reality check applied to it. At this point we might start again with a new alternative or rework options based on the feedback from our stakeholder review.

6. **Keep good records:** key to the success of the Package phase (and in fact the whole P^5 Framework) is good record keeping. When an option is removed from the Package option, a clear record must be kept so that we have an

audit trail of how and why decisions were made throughout the process. This record keeping helps build a body of knowledge that can be invaluable in the future. We can use software tools to help us in this phase. For example, the prioritisation tools from the Prioritise phase or tools to help with data and to visualise results in terms of outcomes such as the financial implications over the next five years, the resourcing implications and how the change impacts on different parts of the business.

7. **Review finances:** often the Package process has a strong financial component because we may be looking at what's affordable. We need to be realistic because if a level of investment is committed, we need to execute and deliver those outcomes for that investment. Many organisations become concerned at this point once they realise the implications. Good financial systems and analysis are essential. This can be a challenge because it requires organisations to look at their costing from an activity-based perspective, which most organisations don't do as a matter of course. We may also want to consider cost 'duplication' between alternatives. When structuring them as hypothetically independent, it may be more realistic to duplicate, say, infrastructure costs. Several alternatives, when considered individually, may require the same infrastructure – all types of aircraft require the same airfield, so when considered alone, the cost of the airfield should be duplicated and included with each

aircraft type. These duplicate costs need taking out at this stage to get to a realistic view – if you are including different aircraft types you may only need a single airfield for all of them.

Think about the Package phase well in advance, what it will look like and the tools and data you will need. This phase is relatively analysis heavy and data oriented. The challenge is for it not to turn into a data game. In fact, you may be thinking that we could entirely automate this phase, particularly as technologies such as artificial intelligence (AI) and machine learning (ML) become more readily accessible. I advocate using sophisticated tools to help manage the complexity of the data. However, as with other phases, the 'human' and social aspects of the Package phase are critical to ensure continued stakeholder ownership and commitment so there should not be any shortcuts.

The Package phase gives the opportunity to get confidence in the package that we are putting forward by looking at different scenarios. A scenario might be a different level of funding or resourcing, or a different strategic environment. We might build several different packages, one for each scenario, and analyse how different each package is within each scenario. The result might be that several alternatives are the same in each package, resulting in a high level of confidence in the work we've done. Therefore, even though we may have considered a single package for a single scenario, we often provide hypothetical scenarios that allow us to test the robustness of the packages we're putting forward. A major government department we worked with were considering at least four scenarios. They found the same alternatives in the top ten of each of those packages. This reinforced their need to focus on that top ten.

Finally, the more we progress, the more tools we can use to help our stakeholders visualise the packages in the operational environment, such as the business or strategic plan, and the more they will engage with these packages. We continue to iterate until we come to a view that the stakeholders are comfortable with, while also maintaining the rigour of the process that's taken us to this point.

JANE'S IT PROJECT PORTFOLIO CHALLENGE

Following Jane's Decision Conference, sensitivity analysis was performed to confirm the robustness of the order of priority. In Jane's case, all the alternatives (the project proposals) were truly independent of each other, so packaging was a short process. Jane and her team worked down the order of priority, starting at the highest value for money, and selected projects until the required resource to deliver them exceeded her team's available resource. Then the proposed package was tested against capital funding budgets and to see that the different parts of the health board were able to take the new solutions on board.

CASE STUDY – HOW DO WE CREATE A SUSTAINABLE DEFENCE FORCE? PART 2

To illustrate the Package phase, we will return to the New Zealand Defence Force (NZDF) who were building an affordable Defence Force in the face of tight financial constraints. In the Package phase, the constraints stakeholders had been given were various future funding scenarios. The Package process started with six different possible funding tracks and a value for money order of priority. The challenge was to turn that into something that met the financial constraints and the financial profile over time and also represented a coherent, practical Defence Force. It became clear that the hypothetical order of priority missed out important parts of the Defence Force and wouldn't work in practice, including some dependency constraints and a number of financial duplications.

The NZDF used sophisticated cost analysis tools to support the Package process. The candidate package options were modelled in the financial analysis tools to check for duplication and ensure costs were realistic. To give key stakeholders confidence in the outcome of the decision once a candidate package was identified, it was re-costed from the ground up to make sure nothing had been missed and that for that level of investment it was possible to deliver that Defence Force.

The results of this work were packages that met the different constraint profiles over time. Trade-offs were made to ensure the Defence Force met all the dependency requirements. Throughout the process, there was a strong participation from the key stakeholders so that what was delivered at the end was well supported. When it was taken back to government, they were satisfied with the level of rigour and the options presented to them.

Avoiding pitfalls

1. **Ignoring the (value for money) order of priority and playing Tetris:** this is tempting, especially when stakeholders become involved in the Packaging process and want to apply their own lens.

2. **Failure to track the consequences of trade-offs:** we may have no record of what alternatives we have given up or gained.

3. **Ignoring the data or over-focus on prioritisation:** the last thing we want is a hypothetically perfect outcome that is unaffordable or unrealistic.

4. **Not allowing enough time in the Package phase:** everyone wants to get to an answer quickly. Make sure there is sufficient time for the analysis required and that the game plan for this phase is followed.

5. **Not checking coherence and deliverability:** it can be easy to build an attractive-looking package that is impractical.

6. **Not involving stakeholders:** it can be tempting to do the packaging in isolation but it's important

to continue to engage with the stakeholders who have participated so far.

Reflection

Consider a major decision you've been involved in or seen being made. Identify the core trade-offs that were made during the decision process:

1. Were the trade-offs explicit and transparent?

2. Was there a clear view of the implications of those trade-offs?

3. Was there a record of the rationale for the trade-offs?

4. What was the core driver for the recommendation?

Summary

The Package phase is where the decision science starts to move into art and considers the wider strategic environment and other organisational considerations. This is an iterative process, in which we start with candidate package options and develop them while accounting for the constraints and dependencies and other broader considerations. It works well if supported by good data, helpful tools and with regular stakeholder check-ins to keep on track. We also need to remain true to the work we have done in the previous three phases.

A clearly planned and well-executed Package phase, in which we iterate and apply reality checks to our initial order of priority, will get us to clear recommendations for the decision that are practical and implementable.

In Chapter 8 we come to the final phase of the P^5 Framework: presenting the outcomes of our decision making to the ultimate decision authority. This may be the last phase, but it is no more or less important than the others.

8
Present

Why present?

In an ideal world, most of the thinking will already have been done in the Plan phase about who the ultimate decision-maker is, what the final decision-making body is and our next steps to reach the committed decision. Once we get past the end of the structured decision-making process and we have a clear recommendation, we have to get clear on what happens next: executing on the decision.

To do this we need to know what other business processes this decision might flow into. Maybe it is an existing formal approval process for investment, a regular strategy process or an annual business planning process. Once we understand that, we can work out how our decision-making process fits within those existing processes. Although much will have been decided in the Plan phase, sometimes the need to press on with our decision overtakes the ability to do complete planning. We may find ourselves asking in the Present phase: who is going to sign off on the decision and what do they need to know to do that? We also need to think about the specific decision point we want to get to. Is it at a committee meeting, a governance meeting, another government process or something of that nature? How will everything we have done so far support the wider aspects around the decision? It can also happen that some of these 'Plan' questions can't be answered until more of the work of the earlier phases is complete and outcomes are emerging.

The Present phase is about turning all the great work we've done in the previous four phases into something that lives in the real world as a decision that then gets executed. Much of what we do in this phase is going to depend entirely on who those end decision-makers are, the other processes in the organisation and any standard documentation that might be required. It may be used for supplementary briefings or for record keeping, for example, and Present is where this information is brought together and made digestible for those who may not have been involved in the decision process to date.

Questions to ask in the Present phase

In this chapter, we'll talk in general terms because making it specific to a particular organisation or decision is very much case by case. However, the same questions can be asked in every case. Many of these may have been answered in the Plan phase or may only become fully apparent now, as Plan intentionally continues in parallel with the other four phases:

1. What is the audience of the end result, for example, the final decision-making body that will commit to the outcome?

2. Who is the accountable decision-maker in that body? This could be the person who signs off on the budget, or the business case. Although we have committees and governance groups and various bodies that consider themselves decision-making bodies, ultimately in any decision process there must be an individual. We need to understand who that individual is. This is a key principle of decision making.

3. In what form does the decision need to be presented so that the person can engage with it?

4. What supporting information might we need to include alongside the decision recommendation?

5. Who else might we want to be involved in Present? We may bring other SMEs or analysts

from elsewhere in the organisation into our process.

Foundations of the Present phase

The four core principles of Decision Thinking apply here, but there are other foundations that are specific to Present:

1. **Begin the Present phase with the end in mind:** before you even start, think about how you will present the result and the decision, who the audience is for that result and what they will need. It may be that the audience is not only the ultimate accountable decision-maker. However, what the audience need and what they want can be two different things. The more you engage directly with the audience, the more you will understand their needs and therefore you will be better able to present to meet those needs. I've got many scars from experiences when advisors have told me what they think the end decision-maker needs and I have missed the mark.

2. **Adhere to academic rigour:** throughout all the phases of the P⁵ Framework, we have generated lots of data and output during the decision process. It can be easy for others within the organisation to take that data out of context. In the Present phase, we need to be cautious about

which data get used and what is inferred from them.

3. **Continuously ensure transparency:** throughout each phase of the P^5 Framework we have ensured strong active stakeholder participation. We need to continue that and not assume that the stakeholders have had their say. Transparency is crucial so that stakeholders can see how their participation in the decision process so far has been represented in a meaningful and valid way.

4. **Less is more:** given all of the work we've done to get to this final phase, it can be tempting to want to include reams of supporting data and information but this can easily obscure the recommendation or the decision we're trying to present. Think carefully about what you leave out as much as what you include.

Present in practice

In the Plan phase, you will have done the planning for your decision-making process. You will know your timeframes but by the time we get to the Present phase the world may have changed or moved on in some way. We need to get clear on any critical milestones in the presentation process. We need to know when the decision or governance body will meet to review our recommendations and we need to meet that deadline.

The Present phase is complete when that presentation of the recommendation is made to the final decision-maker. In many organisations, and particularly in the public sector, there are often several review cycles before the recommendation can even be presented. We have to understand the requirements for those review cycles. Perhaps the governance committee needs papers a week in advance of their meeting or ministers need their briefing two weeks before a Cabinet meeting. Perhaps advisors need to be involved in the briefing before their ministers see the recommendations. It is vital that we get clear on those milestones and their requirements before we start the decision-making process and also on what is expected to come back by way of further recommendations, revisions and requests for information.

The Present phase looks pretty unexciting as it is mostly about documentation. However, this phase is about how we turn all that work we've done into a concise, coherent set of recommendations for our decision-making body. This may now be the time we call upon existing or mandated templates, such as business case templates from within the organisation, so that we present in a way that meets the required existing business processes. While this may feel like the most administrative phase, it is probably the most important because unless we convey the information, the recommendation and the strength of our decision process through the Present phase, all our good work may have been for naught.

There are two keys parts to the Present outcome. The first is the recommendation itself and whatever information supports that recommendation. The second is the documentation and the presentation of the processes we've used to reach that recommendation. This is important as it may be that our end decision-maker has participated in Plan along with other stakeholders and agreed the process we were going to follow. While this is the ideal, it is not always the reality; it may be that you couldn't get access to the decision-maker at that time because they were unavailable or that they rely on their teams to bring recommendations to them.

In this final phase, the decision-maker needs to have confidence in how the recommendation has been reached. The articulation, demonstration and description of the journey to reaching that recommendation can be as important as the actual recommendation itself, particularly if the ultimate decision-maker is a senior stakeholder who could choose to challenge the recommendation. The demonstration of how we've reached the recommendation can be helpful in getting their support.

One might consider the Present phase as where we translate information from our world of structured decision making into the 'ordinary' world of our business or organisation. Because of this we have to think carefully about our language and how we communicate what is important. It may be valuable to involve people with a communications background. I strongly recommend this approach but it comes with a health warning, as it can be tempting for others to want to communicate messages in a style that doesn't relay the reality of the work.

For example, if we are presenting the results of our prioritisation activity with some of the data that relates to the scoring and weighting of our criteria, those numbers have been carefully considered and developed by stakeholders using an academically rigorous process. But it can be tempting to take those numbers out of context, leaving aside the academic rigour, and start giving information that you can't possibly infer from the data. You will remember that in the Package phase we involved experts in decision-making processes and now in the Present phase there is a role for these experts in testing and ensuring that the data that is presented is valid and not misleading. This is not done maliciously but just by those who are over-zealous or lack the knowledge of the end-to-end process and its integrity.

The results of the Present phase are specific to the decision and the nature of that particular business and, therefore, the ultimate decision-maker who is going to sign off on the recommendations. Because of this, the results can be presented in several different ways.

Usually, there is a document that gives the formal recommendation from the outcome of the decision process, which may include an appendix that describes the decision-making process. This is also supported by a presentation pack that is used to brief the decision-making body and allows for a more visual representation of some of the outcomes.

Ultimately, the main output from the Present phase is a clear recommendation and not just a set of alternatives from which the decision-maker makes their choice.

It is also important, as with the other phases of the P^5 Framework, to ensure this is a collaborative process. Including stakeholders is crucial as some may sit on the ultimate decision-making body and may have useful and creative suggestions on how the information and data gathered throughout the decision-making process are presented.

You can also use data analysis or presentation tools to support you in this phase. I urge caution here as the tools should not drive the outcome of the presentation. We need to be clear on what we want to convey in the presentation and then find the tools to help support that. This can be difficult to do once the data is inside some sophisticated business intelligence tool and we realise we can do fascinating things with it but that this may not support the decision; it could, in fact, result in using data, particularly from the Prioritisation phase, in ways that are not valid.

Another reason to involve participants in this phase who have not participated elsewhere in the process is that we may have clear descriptions of our alternatives and clear sets of data that support them, but we might need some wider context that the P^5 Framework work fits within. That context may come from elsewhere in the business or the organisation or even be external to the organisation. We need to think broadly about what's required to make a meaningful presentation from the decision process.

JANE'S IT PROJECT PORTFOLIO CHALLENGE

With an achievable and affordable proposed package complete, Jane presented the recommendation to the IT governance board, presenting the order of priority, the list of projects being recommended to proceed with and those being recommended to delay or remove. The presentation also included details on the value the proposed portfolio would deliver against the criteria. The IT governance board accepted the recommendations and the portfolio was approved. Jane immediately started delivering on the projects, safe in the knowledge that the stakeholders fully supported the project delivery plan.

CASE STUDY – HOW TO MAKE A GOVERNMENT SECTOR SUSTAINABLE?

A group of government agencies who were working together on a long-term sustainable future for their sector used a rigorous decision process based on the P^5 Framework. Stakeholders were fully engaged and a lot of detailed data was gathered and analysed. Future possible outcomes were generated in the Package phase. In the Present phase, the challenge was how to put all of this information together for the ultimate ministerial decision authority – the Cabinet – so that they could engage meaningfully with the content. The team responsible for the decision process needed to strike a delicate balance between oversimplifying the information so that it lost credibility and overcomplicating it so that time-poor senior ministers couldn't engage with it.

To ensure they got this balance right, they allowed sufficient time for the Present phase. From the Plan phase the team were clear on what the review cycles and milestones were and when the ultimate recommendation would go to the Cabinet and the Prime Minister and, with that in mind, started the Present phase with a creative process to look at different formats.

They started looking at standard Cabinet paper formats but realised that the significance and complexity of this decision needed something more creative. They devised an A3 place-mat type format, where each of the packages developed under the Package phase was presented on a single sheet of A3 paper. That page contained details of the alternatives included in the package and those that were excluded, the priorities and the value outcomes against the criteria, and the risks government would be exposed to by taking this package. Also included were visual representations that indicated the geographic consequences. It became clear during the Present phase that a single A3 at the top bringing together all three packages into one view was needed so that the Cabinet could see at a glance how the packages related to each other.

During the Present phase it sometimes becomes clear that there is a decision process within a decision process. In this case study, three proposed packages were being put forward for the Cabinet to decide on. Given that the key output from the Present phase is to make a clear recommendation, in this instance the paperwork made a recommendation of the proposed preferred package and made clear the trade-offs if a different package was selected. This was a smart move because, ultimately, the Cabinet were the decision-making body and they needed the freedom to make their decision with the full knowledge of all the available information. The challenge was to provide enough information for the Cabinet to make that decision and not feel they were being railroaded. Getting this right takes careful planning and thinking through during the Present phase.

Presenting each option on an A3 sheet, beneath one overarching A3 that showed how the different packages compared to each other, was a clear and easy way for ministers to engage and see why one package might be preferred over another and what the consequences of picking one package over another were. The information was well received by the Cabinet, who made a clear decision on the recommendations and gave positive feedback about the format of the information presented and the ease with which they could see the different dimensions of the decision, how the decision had been made and the rigour of the decision process.

Avoiding pitfalls

1. **Not knowing your audience:** building the presentation of the recommendation in a form that is not expected by the audience can cause delays and challenges to commitment. There is no need to reinvent the wheel – do what works in other processes that have a similar audience.

2. **Pressure from people who have not been involved in the process:** they may request that the recommendation communicates certain intentions. We need to be cautious that we're not trying to use the work throughout the structured decision process to serve ends for which it was not intended or designed. We can all imagine how, in the political sphere, this might be the case. Going back to the four core principles, we need to watch how the data gets presented and the conclusions that are drawn from the data, particularly as it is tempting to do mischief once the breadth and richness of what has been generated is seen.

3. **Losing stakeholder ownership:** unlike the other phases of the P^5 Framework, where it is clear how active stakeholder participation can take place, in the Present phase it is not so obvious where stakeholder participation fits. One way is to share drafts of the output of this phase with stakeholder groups and engage them in creative conversations to shape the output. We also

want a clear narrative on how the stakeholders participated in reaching the decision so that there is no question about the level of support and ownership that the stakeholders have had. Resist the temptation to make the information shared with stakeholders too brief as stakeholders may become disenfranchised after the decision.

4. **Overloading the recommendation:** given that there is so much richness to all the work that we've done, it is tempting to turn our recommendation from what might be a ten-slide PowerPoint presentation and a three-page document into a version of *War and Peace*.

Reflection

Consider a senior decision-making body in your organisation, which might be an investment committee or similar:

1. How can the output of a structured decision-making process be presented in a way that meets the requirements of the standard reporting?

2. Who is the ultimate decision-maker there? Reflect on what their needs might be to help them to make the decision confidently.

Summary

The Present phase is about getting to the ultimate decision, having the right information in the hands of the decision-making body.

Typically, the presentation will be in several different formats to suit the end audience, which could be standard or templated and will include both the recommendation and some detail of the process by which it was reached to give confidence in it.

Finally, a key part of the Present phase is understanding the timeframes that we need to meet for review and sign-off processes so that our effort throughout the P⁵ Framework isn't lost by missing a critical deadline.

Developing a clear presentation of the decision recommendation in a style and language that meets the ultimate decision authority's expectations will give us a high chance of approval – and of our decision sticking.

Conclusion

Let's bring together everything we've learned about making hard decisions easy and having them stick using a structured decision process based on the P⁵ Decision Framework. We started with the fact that decision making is a discipline. A whole world of science, processes, tools and skills exists around it. We also know that better decision making involves a transparent process, getting strong commitment to the outcome and that stakeholder engagement is crucial to its success – this is Decision Thinking.

There are four key principles to structured decision making:

- **Process before content:** get the decision process designed, written down and signed off before you jump into making the decision. This will set you up for success and ensure that your stakeholders are in agreement before you get into the contentious material.

- **Academic rigour:** use academically founded processes so that when you start to consider numbers and the mix of psychological and mathematical impacts, you can do this in a way that is valid and can be relied on should your decision ever be challenged.

- **Active stakeholder participation:** engage with stakeholders and encourage them to participate throughout your decision process in an active way wherever possible.

- **Intangible and tangible value:** look at every aspect of value impacted by the decision – not just what we can measure, such as dollars.

Here's a recap of each phase of the P^5 Decision Framework that is founded on these four principles:

1. **Plan:** design the process and identify the who, what, why, when and how of the decision. Although we talk of Plan as being the first phase, planning continues throughout our decision process. It is key at the end of Plan to get agreement to the decision process you're going to follow.

2. **Prepare:** the first part of this phase is to develop criteria for our decision making. What are the outcomes it will provide? What does value look like? What are the risks? These need to be clearly articulated and agreed by stakeholders. The second part of the Prepare phase is to formulate our alternatives. Articulate them clearly with requisite data to support them and agree them with stakeholders.

3. **Prioritise:** look at our alternatives through the lens of our criteria and assess which ones provide more or less value than others so that we end up with an order of priority. Use a technical process such as MCDA for modelling the decision and use group or social processes, such as Decision Conferencing, to actively engage with stakeholders in this phase.

4. **Package:** this is when the science meets the art of decision making and we start to make practical sense of our order of priority by looking at different combinations of alternatives to deliver the overall outcomes for our decision.

5. **Present:** present our decision within our approval processes in our organisation. We need to make sure that what we provide meets the needs of our ultimate decision-maker.

What action can you take right now?

You may now be asking yourself what action you can take to improve how decisions are made in your organisation. I recommend that you review the four core principles of Decision Thinking immediately and decide on one action you can take for each principle that would have an immediate impact on the quality of a decision you are facing or are expecting to face in the future.

Principle 1: process before content

Write down the five major steps in the process for reaching that decision, starting with the last step first and working backwards.

Principle 2: academic rigour

Note the key items of data you might need to support your decision, for example, performance or environmental data. Then categorise those data as:

1. Constraints that we can't exceed or must not forget.

2. Data that directly represents the value it provides to.

3. Data that we may need to score in our prioritisation process, where the value we get from that information isn't the data itself.

Principle 3: active stakeholder participation

List all the stakeholders who will be impacted by the decision. Think broadly and then categorise them on a scale of one to four, where one is the most impacted and four is the least impacted.

Principle 4: intangible and tangible value

List the ways in which the decision provides value. Start with what is tangible and then keep asking why this decision is important. Look at the stakeholder list that you've just written and ask yourself what value would look like to them, perhaps starting with Category 1 stakeholders.

If you work through those four key actions for a decision you expect to face in the future, I can guarantee that the quality of your decision outcome will be better. If you follow this link – harddecisionsmadeeasy.com/worksheet – you can download a simple worksheet that includes these actions.

By taking these actions you will have a better understanding of the quality of decision making in your organisation right now. To help you further with this we have put together an online Decision Quality Diagnostic. Follow this link to access the tool: harddecisionsmadeeasy.com/diagnostic. It will take you through a series of questions and will show you the places that need attention in your current decision-making process.

We have explored the P⁵ Framework in great detail in this book, and as a ready reference, you can find a PDF version with a little more detail here: harddecisionsmadeeasy.com/p5.

If you would like further support with your decisions, please find my contact details on The Author page at the back of the book.

I'm excited to know that you are committed to transforming the way you and your organisation make decisions and am glad to have helped you on your way. Good luck!

References

Axelos, 'Management of portfolios', www.axelos.
com/best-practice-solutions/mop, accessed 3
February 2021

Beheshti, N, '10 Timely statistics about the connection
between employee engagement and wellness',
Forbes (16 January 2019), www.forbes.com/sites/
nazbeheshti/2019/01/16/10-timely-statistics-about-
the-connection-between-employee-engagement-and-
wellness/?sh=2e06c4622a03, accessed 3 February
2021

Business Roundtable, 'Business Roundtable
redefines the purpose of a corporation to promote
"an economy that serves all Americans"' (19 August

2019), www.businessroundtable.org/business-roundtable-redefines-the-purpose-of-a-corporation-to-promote-an-economy-that-serves-all-americans, accessed 3 February 2021

Cloverpop.com, 'Hacking diversity with inclusive decision making' (2017), www.cloverpop.com/hubfs/Whitepapers/Cloverpop_Hacking_Diversity_Inclusive_Decision_Making_White_Paper.pdf, accessed 3 February 2021

Coleman, J, speech to the Defence Industry Association annual conference, Wellington, New Zealand (2013)

Covey, RS, *The 7 Habits of Highly Effective People: Powerful lessons in personal change* (Free Press, 1989)

Dictionary.com, 'Trade-off', www.dictionary.com/browse/trade-off, accessed 3 February 2021

Dodgson, J, Spackman, M, Pearman, A and Phillips, L, *Multi-Criteria Analysis: A manual*, Department of the Environment, Transport and the Regions (2000; republished 2009 by the Department for Communities and Local Government)

Glassdoor Team, 'New survey: Company mission & culture matter more than salary' (11 July 2019), www.glassdoor.co.uk/blog/mission-culture-survey, accessed 3 February 2021

Kahneman, D, *Thinking Fast and Slow* (Farrar, Straus and Giroux, 2011)

Keeney, RL, *Value-Focused Thinking: A path to creative decision making* (Harvard University Press, 1992)

Ocean Tomo, 'Intangible asset market value study' (7 January 2020), www.oceantomo.com/intangible-asset-market-value-study, accessed 7 February 2021

Phillips, LD, 'A theory of requisite decision models', *Acta Psychologica* (1984), 56: 29–48

Phillips, LD, 'Decision conferencing'. In Edwards, W, Miles, RF and von Winterfeldt, D (eds), *Advances in Decision Analysis: From foundations to applications* (Cambridge University Press, 2007)

Phillips, LD, 'Requisite decision modelling: A case study', *The Journal of the Operational Research Society* (1982), 33: 303–11

Phillips, LD, 'The Royal Navy's Type 45 story: A case study'. In Salo, A, Keisler, J and Morton, A (eds), *Portfolio Decision Analysis: Improved methods for resource allocation* (Springer, 2011)

Ponczek, S, 'Epic S&P 500 rally is powered by assets you can't see or touch', *Bloomberg* (21 October 2020), www.bloomberg.com/news/articles/2020-10-21/epic-s-p-500-rally-is-powered-by-assets-you-can-t-see-or-touch, accessed 3 February 2021

Raiffa, H, *Decision Analysis: Introductory lectures on choices under uncertainty* (Addison-Wesley, 1968)

Sorkin, AR, 'BlackRock's message: Contribute to society, or risk losing our support', *The New York Times* (2018) www.nytimes.com/2018/01/15/business/dealbook/blackrock-laurence-fink-letter.html, accessed 3 February 2021

Useem, J, 'Jim Collins on tough calls', *Fortune* (2005), https://archive.fortune.com/magazines/fortune/fortune_archive/2005/06/27/8263408/index.htm, accessed 3 February 2021

Acknowledgements

M any people might say this book has been a long time coming, and it is likely I may never have written it were it not for the awesome people around me – providing input, support, encouragement, critique and also time and space. Thank you, thank you, thank you!

First and foremost, thanks so much to my amazing family – my wife Joanna and my two superhero boys, Fox and Maverick – for your unwavering and unconditional support and cheerleading, not just as I was writing this book, but in everything I do. There were many times when it seemed all too hard, and you always helped re-energise me. You're the best and I love you so much.

To my extraordinary team at Catalyze APAC: Belinda Newham, Don Gomez, Edward Poot, Jess Oses, Shona Bernard Chandler and Tapio Sorsa. Thank you for joining me on this journey to transform decision making in the world and for all the hard work, help, insights and opinions that have made this book a reality – and for making sure I set the time aside!

Larry Phillips, without you and your non-stop energy and commitment, not only would this book not exist, but perhaps even the entire subject matter might not exist! You have been such an inspiration to me throughout my work in decision making and you have always kept it grounded in rigorous science. Thank you so much for your amazing support, your review of the manuscript, your detailed references and, above all, your desire to also see a world that works through structured, collaborative decision making.

Rhys Jones – thank you so much for writing such a powerful and meaningful foreword. It was a real privilege to work for you as a client, see your leadership in action and the great results you achieved from it. I'm honoured to have your words open my book.

To Kevin Bossley, thank you for being the catalyst for my entrepreneurial journey all those years ago, taking the leap with me and nudging me as we leapt! Also, huge thanks for your detailed review and feedback on the manuscript – your breadth and depth of experience in supporting decision making and really bringing structured decision making to life is unique.

Anthony Ween, your review of the manuscript, detailed and helpful suggestions and general input and discussion have been fantastic, thank you (not to mention your expertise in beer, but that's for another book). As someone who has really put a lot of this work into practice in the public sector, your first-hand experience was invaluable.

Patrick Sharry, much of what I know as a facilitator of social processes I've learned from you, so your review of the manuscript as both a like-minded practitioner of these techniques and your encyclopaedic knowledge of business books was superb – thank you! Your knowledge and passion for wine is also exceptional but that, too, is for another book.

Thank you, Joanne Hutchinson for your very helpful review and reflections on the manuscript – your perspective as someone who has been involved in social decision processes as a senior public servant was critical to the book.

Emily-Lee Waldao, Nina James and Joanna Marsh, it has been fantastic working with you and Investa as forward-looking clients; your help and input with the case studies in the book really brings it to life, thank you.

I can't forget team Catalyze UK, and especially thanks to you, Bob Kitchen; without us meeting all those years ago, I would never have embarked on this amazing journey. Thank you for all your experience and guidance and for the great work you are all doing putting this into practice.

Many thanks to Daryl Charles for the great work on my author photos; you have such an eye for light and seem to be able to work miracles making me look presentable!

Massive thanks to Glen Carlson and the team at Dent; your Key Person of Influence programme was instrumental in capturing and articulating the ideas in this book – and inspired me to make my own dent in the Universe!

Finally, huge thanks to the fantastic team at Rethink Press. In particular to Siobhan Costello for your commitment and consistent support as I wrote the manuscript and to Eve Makepeace for really holding my hand through the publishing process and being ever-helpful and ever-responsive. And not forgetting Lucy McCarraher; it was your early webinars that showed me that writing a book could be a reality and was actually within reach.

The Author

Paul Gordon is an accomplished strategist and expert communicator who has successfully designed, implemented and facilitated decision processes across the globe that have impacted millions of people. His diverse client base includes national defence forces and intelligence agencies, victim support organisations, large corporate investors, critical infrastructure providers and multi-national corporations.

Paul thrives on the possibility of better decision-making to propel improved outcomes and is a passionate advocate of collaborative process design and execution. He has a vision for a world where everyone is engaged in decisions that matter to them, and where conscious, structured, inclusive decision-making is the norm.

As CEO of Catalyze APAC, Paul leads a team of experts to support some of the most powerful decision-makers in Australia, New Zealand, and the broader pacific region. Their application of Decision Thinking transforms strategy development, portfolio selection, option analysis and prioritisation, while building client capability that drives whole-of-organisation performance.

Paul lives with his wife and young family in Sydney, Australia, where he enjoys sailing, fine food and wine, CrossFit and honing his vocals as a member of a local choir.

Paul welcomes connections via the following links.

⊕ www.harddecisionsmadeeasy.com

⊕ www.catalyzeapac.com

▥ www.linkedin.com/in/decisions

✉ paulgordon@catalyzeapac.com

Printed in Australia
AUHW021204111121
355155AU00009B/9

9 781781 335710